Blue-Collar Soldiers?

To My Wife

Alan Ned Sabrosky

Blue-Collar Soldiers?

Unionization and the U.S. Military

Westview Press
Boulder, Colorado

WESTVIEW SPECIAL STUDIES IN MILITARY AFFAIRS
A Foreign Policy Research Institute Book

Published 1978 in the United States of America by
       Westview Press, Inc.
       5500 Central Avenue
       Boulder, Colorado 80301
       Frederick A. Praeger, Publisher and Editorial Director

LIBRARY OF CONGRESS CATALOGING IN PUBLICATION DATA
Main entry under title:

Blue-collar soldiers?

     Includes index.
     1. Military unions—United States—Addresses,
essays, lectures.   I. Sabrosky, Alan N.
UH743.B59   331.88'11'35500973   77-13018

 ISBN 0−89158−055−7

Printed and bound in the United States of America

CONTENTS

Foreword   *William R. Kintner*   vii

1.   Blue-Collar Soldiers? The Question of American
     Military Unionization
     Alan Ned Sabrosky   1

2.   Issues in Military Unionization
     William J. Taylor, Jr.   11

3.   For A Brotherhood of Men-at-Arms: The Case for
     Military Unionization
     Gene Phillips   55

4.   The Case against Military Unionization
     David Y. Denholm and *Theodore C. Humes*   69

5.   Public Sector Unionization and the U.S. Military:
     A First Amendment Issue
     Charles D. Phillips and *Judith A. Crosby*   89

6.   The Implications of European Military Unions for the
     United States Armed Forces
     Ezra S. Krendel   109

7.   American Military Unions: A Sociological Analysis
     Thomas C. Wyatt   125

8.   Military Unionism in America: Retrospect and Prospect
     Alan Ned Sabrosky   143

Appendix A   Agenda: Executive Conference on Unionization
             and the U.S. Military (Philadelphia, Pa.,
             April 22, 1977)   159

Appendix B   S.274 (January 18, 1977)   161

Index   165

FOREWORD

Few would deny that the premises underlying American national security policy have been subjected to increasing pressure in recent years. Many questions have been raised, and too few answers provided, concerning the proper linkage of power and purpose in American foreign policy. Yet, unless our capabilities are brought into harmony with our commitments, unless we acquire a clear understanding of the relationship of those capabilities to the exercise of influence in world affairs, our long-term security will be problematical at best.

Recognizing the importance of this issue, the Foreign Policy Research Institute has initiated a two-year study on the subject of "Strategic Choices and Military Power." This book on military unionism is the first product of that research program. It provides a balanced and timely assessment of the constitutionality, feasibility and desirability of military unions in the United States. As such, it should go far toward improving our understanding of this complex and significant subject.

William R. Kintner
President

ACKNOWLEDGMENTS

Perhaps even more than the author of a book, an editor owes a considerable debt of gratitude to many people. The support and encouragement of my colleagues at the Foreign Policy Research Institute played an essential part in the planning and completion of this project. Mr. G. Dennis Bolton, Mrs. Judith Flanagan and Mr. William C. Ellenbogen assisted in the organization of an executive conference on "Unionization and the U.S. Military," sponsored by the Institute in April 1977. Professor Edward Bernard Glick of Temple University, Professor David R. Segal of the University of Maryland and Mr. Virgel E. Miller of the American Federation of Government Employees provided perceptive comments on many different aspects of military unionism. Mr. Charles B. Purrenhage supervised the transformation of an unedited manuscript into a finished work with extraordinary patience and skill. Mrs. Jean Barth Tobin copy-edited the manuscript; Mrs. Carmena Pyfrom and Ms. Valerie Garner diligently and bravely typed the many drafts of the edited papers; Mr. Alan H. Luxenberg and Mr. Joseph Woods assisted in more ways than can fully be appreciated; and a special note of appreciation must be given to Ms. Donna Reese, who set the copy into camera-ready pages for printing.

Finally, thanks are due the authors of the papers assembled in this volume. Each author, of course, is responsible for the factual accuracy of the evidence presented in his or her chapter. In addition, when editing these papers, I endeavored (not always, I fear, with complete success!) to resist the perennial temptation to make each one say something the way the editor himself would like it said. In many ways, the strength of these contributions reflects their resilience under the editorial pen. Taken together, I believe they provide many useful insights into an issue of continuing importance to students and practitioners of American national security affairs.

Alan Ned Sabrosky
September 1977

Chapter One
BLUE-COLLAR SOLDIERS? THE QUESTION OF AMERICAN MILITARY UNIONIZATION

by Alan Ned Sabrosky

The ultimate test of any institution is its ability to meet successfully the ever-changing demands that are placed upon it, adapting as necessary to preserve its essential structural and functional integrity. Few institutions, however, have been so ill-prepared to deal with a major challenge as the American military when confronted with the prospect of unionization. While still in the process of disengaging from the traumatic experience of the Indochina conflict, the United States had decided to end peacetime conscription and to rely instead entirely on volunteers to meet the manpower requirements of the armed forces. This was a controversial measure, indeed. Although the armed forces had retained a greater measure of public confidence in the course of the Vietnam experience than many other American institutions, they, too, had been subjected to a wide range of disruptive influences. Many of the traditional patterns of authority and management no longer commanded widespread acceptance, either within the government and the society in general, or in the military establishment itself. The effort to create an all-volunteer force (AVF) was therefore a clear attempt to eliminate the source of much of the discontent that had beset the armed services during the combined peaks of antiwar dissension and urban rioting. In this way, it was believed, the military could reforge the institutional cohesiveness essential to the maintenance of an effective defense establishment.

The services, however, have enjoyed only mixed success in their endeavor. It is becoming increasingly clear that the all-volunteer force is neither so great a success as its proponents had anticipated, nor so great a failure as its opponents had feared. Substantial progress had been made toward overcoming some of the most corrosive aspects of the institutional deterioration that had set in during the course of the Indochina conflict. Yet it is equally clear that the defense establishment is still far from being the efficient, professional, and highly motivated force portrayed by its senior military and civilian officials. Clear improvements have been registered, but serious questions remain about the present status and future viability of the all-volunteer force concept.

On balance, it seems that the defense establishment is still in large measure a transitional force capable of either further improvement or a renewed decline. To facilitate that improvement, or at least stave off a decline, the military needs nothing so much as a respite from major external and internal stress. Unfortunately, that respite may not be forthcoming. The services are now faced with yet another challenge to institutional stability, cohesion, and traditions. That challenge is the increasing attention being given to the prospects for the unionization of the armed forces. And whatever the objective merits of military unionism, there is no doubt that the transitional character of the existing all-volunteer force inhibits the ability of the armed services to meet this challenge promptly and effectively.

The potential for American military unionization had existed for some time, of course. The unionization of several Western European defense establishments had shown that armed forces were not necessarily a preserve into which trade unions could not go. Closer to home, the unionization of increasing numbers of so-called public service employees (such as teachers, hospital staffs, and governmental workers) demonstrated that the American labor movement had no intention of limiting itself to the private sector. The formation of police and fire department unions in many states and localities underscored the point that the unionization of public safety personnel, whether or not they were armed, at one level of government could portend, or even legitimize, the unionization of the armed forces themselves. Widespread discontent in the military during the Vietnam War, especially among draftees, had led at one point to the creation of a short-lived American Servicemen's Union (ASU). Even a "union of military physicians" had made its appearance in 1975 among American medical officers stationed in Western Europe with the U.S. Seventh Army. Finally, the uncertainties attending the all-volunteer force itself had led the defense establishment to adopt a number of recruiting and manpower management practices that helped provide a basis on which pro-union sentiment could grow.

Under these circumstances, it would have been surprising if one or more unions had *not* expressed an interest in organizing armed forces personnel. And in fact, the "military unionization" movement is far from monolithic. The efforts of the American Federation of Government Employees (AFGE), an affiliate of the AFL-CIO, are perhaps best known. If a poll of the AFGE membership now under way approves the AFGE's governing council's decision to enroll servicemen, that union will probably have a commanding lead over any of its actual or potential competitors. Yet other groups also are interested in unionizing the military. Between them, for example, the National Association of Government Employees

(NAGE) and the Association of Civilian Technicians (ACT) have organized at least sixteen thousand technicians and employees in National Guard and reserve forces of most of the states. At least one of these unions (ACT) reportedly has signed up active-duty personnel as well; both *could* do so. The Teamsters and Maritime Workers' unions once contemplated recruiting military personnel, and are still considered to be interested in doing so despite public disclaimers by their leadership. A group known as the "Enlisted People's Organizing Committee" (EPOC), which advocates a "democratic" union exclusively for lower-ranking enlisted personnel, is on the hustings, as are a number of other activist groups which advocate various types of more politicized, and often radicalized, American military unions.

Two conclusions seem inescapable at this time. First, the issue of military unionization is neither an academic question nor a fantasy concocted by alarmists. It is a very real possibility that is being advocated or studied by a number of diverse groups, finds a surprising degree of support within the armed services on the basis of preliminary surveys of army and air force personnel, and is most unlikely to disappear of its own volition. Second, there is little doubt that military unions would have a considerable impact on the military institution as a whole, as well as the character of civil-military relations in this country. Precisely what that impact would be, however, is uncertain. The issues involved are complex, the arguments on both sides of the debate are many, and the consequences of American military unions for the functional effectiveness and political responsiveness of the armed forces are uncertain.

The complexity of the debate on American military unionism is outlined in Chapter Two in "Issues in Military Unionization" by Colonel William J. Taylor, Jr. Colonel Taylor, a member of the permanent faculty at the U.S. Military Academy, presents a balanced view of the general arguments for and against the key issues. As he sees it, six issues are central to an assessment of the implications of military unions for the United States. These issue-areas are: (1) societal trends and public employee unions, (2) diverse views on the unionization of the military, (3) relevant analogies, (4) impact of unions on military effectiveness, (5) constitutional rights and military membership in unions, and (6) alternatives to military unionization.

Colonel Taylor concludes that, to the extent there is a significant movement toward military unionization, the reasons for it are couched in general societal trends and in the state of the volunteer force under the present national economy. Within the military, arguments that there has been an erosion in both material and individual "rights," and that existing mechanisms for promoting "justice" for service personnel are inadequate have laid a foundation of support for military unions. The public seems opposed to military unions, although that opposition may be decreasing, especially among those in the eighteen-to-twenty-four age group and racial minorities. Congress still seems inclined to oppose military unions, but its eventual position cannot be predicted with certainty. There is growing interest by public unions in signing up the military, with the AFGE in particular believing that military unionization is not only feasible, but inevitable. European military unions may not be analogous to those that might appear in the United States, due to the different societal contexts involved. The impact of military unions on the effectiveness of the armed services is uncertain; both advantages and disadvantages could ensue simultaneously, with mixed consequences for the military. The constitutionality of broadly based statutes either supporting or prohibiting military unions would probably be upheld by the Supreme Court, although the Court has tended to subordinate the First Amendment rights of military personnel to the requirements of military necessity. Finnally, it is possible that it is already too late to prevent the eventual unionization of the military, although that is certainly not inevitable. A program of compulsory national service (CNS) might be the only viable alternative both for solving the problems of the all-volunteer force and for obviating the rationale for military unionization.

While Colonel Taylor's carefully documented analysis shows why the debate on American military unions is far from being resolved, the arguments in Chapters Three and Four demonstrate why that debate is unlikely to be reconciled easily, if at all. Those chapters are clearly advocacy papers presenting, respectively, the cases for and against the unionization of the U.S. armed forces. As such, they do not presume to take a balanced view of the subject. That this should be so may be profoundly disturbing to some scholars. Yet the apparent irreconcilability and selective use of evidence and issues in these chapters are illustrative of the crux of the current problem. For as the reader will quickly see, the cases for and against American military unions rest on different premises, view different issues to be of central importance, and—at the very least—draw different inferences and conclusions from the same body of evidence. The importance of this divergence of opinion cannot be overestimated. If the debate on military unionization is to be resolved at all, it will be decided not on the basis of balanced, objective analyses, but as a function of the interaction of contending parties who reject the fundamental legitimacy of each other's position and are concerned solely with marshaling support for their far from unbiased and impartial positions.

The significance of this is immediately apparent in Chapter Three. In "For a Brotherhood of Men-at-Arms," Colonel Gene Phillips—

himself a retired army officer who has counseled the AFGE in its deliberations on military unionization—sees the issue of military unions in unambiguous terms. American military unions, in his opinion, are a matter of simple justice due those who bear arms in a democratic society. Colonel Phillips emphasizes the importance of linking military service with the full and unabridged rights of citizenship. Those who oppose military unions do so, he believes, only out of a hypocritical and ill-conceived acceptance of an invalid "conventional wisdom." Only one argument against military unions is conceded to have "an undeniable element of truth." This is the concern that a military union would demand a voice in foreign affairs, and, in those instances where its view differed from that of the administration, the apparent fissure in our national solidarity could weaken the credibility of the cheif executive in his dealings with other governments. Such a fear, however, is seen to be unduly exaggerated. Colonel Phillips observes that the president often has acted abroad, and acted successfully, without having a clear and unambiguous base of domestic support. Any ambivalence in America's image abroad that might follow the unionization of the armed forces could therefore be tolerated. But more to the point, the author asserts that the record of the American Federation of Government Employees, as well as the public and private statements of its leaders, leaves no doubt that it intends to limit its concerns to the social and economic inequities existing in the armed services. The union, he contends, will leave foreign policy to those branches of government entrusted with its keeping.

Like most advocates of military unions, Colonel Phillips is sensitive to the charge of critics such as Senator Strom Thurmond that unionization would undermine the effectiveness and reliability of the armed forces. In his paper he argues forcefully that unionization would not affect adversely the performance of the armed services. On the contrary, he argues that it actually would improve them. The principle value of a military union to the manager in the armed forces, in his opinion, is the degree of self-discipline that a union would impose on its members. A military union also would reinforce what he sees to be the basic objective of military management, ·whether in garrison or in the field: the pursuit of justice, tempered with compassion and respect for human dignity. Moreover, Colonel Phillips considers military unions to be important facilitators of communication between management and the work force—the heart, in his opinion, of both military leadership and good labor relations. A labor union steward as a member of the "brotherhood of men-at-arms," for example, would be simply another legitimate means for commanders to use in communicating with the personnel in their units. In this regard, a military union would strengthen rather than usurp the chain of command. Finally, Colonel Phillips contends that the ultimate reason for a military union in America is that there is no moral justification for our society to deny this right to those of its citizens in the military who wish to unionize.

In many respects, Colonel Phillips' argument on behalf of military unionization is compelling. Certainly, if the link connecting moral necessity, constitutional legitimacy, and military utility was as strong and clear as he suggests, a rational person would find it difficult *not* to support the military union movement in this country. Yet as David Y. Denholm and Theodore C. Humes show in Chapter Four, there is clearly a different perspective to be entertained on the question. The authors, both of whom are affiliated with the Public Service Research Council, acknowledge in "The Case against Military Unionization" that moral and constitutional considerations are important in the debate. They make it equally clear, however, that there are also a number of very different political issues involved as well, and that these argue strongly against the unionization of the U.S. military. Denholm and Humes take pains to point out that military unionism is not a subject to be taken lightly. To act on the assumption that opposition to military unions is so widespread that unionization would never occur could well be counterproductive and self-defeating. The surest way to prevent military unionism from becoming a reality, they argue, is to legislate the strongest possible restrictions against it. These prohibitions, in their opinion, are entirely within the power of the Congress and consistent with the constitutional rights assigned to military personnel.

Denholm and Humes differ totally with Colonel Phillips on the impact of military unions on the armed forces. They contend that unionism in the U.S. military is contrary to the public interest because of the detrimental effects it would have on the national defense, the political processes, and democratic traditions of this country. They observe that a union in a collective bargaining relationship has but one function: to obtain from the employer more than the employer is willing to give voluntarily. The decisions on how and where to get the "more" for a union's members are essentially political decisions, when the union involved is in the public sector. Moreover, a union is a political entity whose leadership's position depends on its ability to exact gains from management in excess of whatever management is prepared to offer. And the only truly meaningful argument that a union has at the bargaining table is the withdrawal *en masse* of the services of its members—in short, a strike or job action of some type. It is all too clear, in their opinion, that neither the fact nor the threat of a strike could be tolerated within any military establishment that considered efficiency to be important, yet strikes are inherent in unions, and would be so in a military union. Finally, there is no reason to believe that a military union would not be as politically active as any other union. The unionization of the military would therefore have as its natural consequence the politicization of the military, with all of the problems that would pose for our democratic system of government.

Regardless of the rationale for and against the unionization of the U.S. armed forces, there is little doubt that the constitutionality of American military unions would be tested in the courts. The fact that both advocates and opponents of military unions see the issue of military unions in large measure as a constitutional question suggests that any vote or legislation on unionization would be challenged by the side whose view had not prevailed at that point. The constitutionality of American military unions as part of the public sector is addressed by Mr. Charles D. Phillips of the Federal Judicial Center and Professor Judith A. Crosby of Gallaudet College in "Public Sector Unionization and the U.S. Military: A First Amendment Issue" in Chapter Five. The fundamental constitutional issue in military unionization is, in their view, which provision of the Constitution is paramount: Congress' powers to regulate the military, or the First Amendment rights of military personnel? Four types of congressional action on the question of military unionization are seen to be possible. Congress could: (1) prohibit military unionization, denying the right to join in addition to the rights to bargain and to strike; (2) prohibit bargaining and striking, but authorize joining a union; (3) prohibit striking, while authorizing joining and collective bargaining; or (4) place no restrictions on the rights of military personnel to unionize. Yet they acknowledge that *any* statuatory action the Congress takes here will be tested in the Supreme Court. Thus, the key question is really how the Court is likely to rule on the fundamental constitutional issues involved.

The authors, while recognizing the difficulties inherent in trying to predict how the Supreme Court will rule on any issue, conclude that the Court as it is presently constituted would probably rule that : (1) Congress has the constitutional authority to prohibit military unionization; (2) the First Amendment associational rights of military personnel may be infringed; and (3) the Congress may broadly prohibit unionization of military personnel through even as wide-ranging a statute as S. 3079 introduced by Senator Thurmond in 1976. The present Supreme Court also would uphold any constitutional statute restricting, but not prohibiting, the unionization of military personnel. Future Courts, they concede, might not act in a similar fashion .

The final caveat in the Phillips-Crosby paper raises an important point. The constitutionality or unconstitutionality of anything is never a closed subject. Different Courts, at different times, have upheld the constitutionality of segregated education that was "seperate but equal," and subsequently ruled that what was separate could never be constitutionally equal. Similarly, a Court ruling denying the constitutionality of military unions does not preclude the possibility that a subsequent Court could rule in a very different fashion, and vice versa. Thus, we cannot overlook the possibility that American military unions might one day become a reality, regardless of any legislation or Court decisions made in the near future. And if military unions might one day make their appearance in this country, what impact would they be likely to have on the U.S. military and the society it serves?

Broadly speaking, two possible analogies to American military unions could be said to exist. These are military unions in the political democracies of Western Europe, and the union movement—particularly in the public sector—in the United States itself. Both advocates and opponents of American military unions draw on the European experience with military unions. The fact that they reach diametrically opposite conclusions about the impact of military unions, although relying on the same body of evidence, says much about the complexity of the debate. Yet having said this, *are* such analogies relevant to the American situation? Professor Ezra S. Krendel of the University of Pennsylvania looks at this question in Chapter Six, "The Implications of European Military Unions for the United States Armed Forces," with results that may disconcert some on both sides of the issue.

The first thing that must be recognized, in the author's opinion, is that European military unions are part of a labor movement that differs in significant ways from American trade unionism. In fact, he suggests, there is no American "labor movement," civilian or military, in the European sense. In addition, the most significant and inescapable distinction between the European military experience with trade unionism and analogies with the armed forces of the United States lies in the difference in the strategic roles of the respective forces. Put bluntly, hesitation in the command and control activities or a lapse in the effectiveness of the combat arms would be of far greater significance in the American armed forces than in those of any or all of the European democracies. It can also be argued, he believes, that military unions in the context of American society would create the potential for inducing a "Praetorian Guard" attitude on the part of their members rather than provide a means of institutionalizing the influence of civilian democratic traditions in the armed forces as in certain European states.

After summarizing the performance of military unions in Norway, the Netherlands, West Germany, and Sweden, Professor Krendel suggests that four inferences may be drawn from the European experience. First, far from being an anomaly, military unions evolve from the orderly maturation of public sector collective bargaining, of which they are a logical conclusion. Second, "new left" activist efforts at organizing soldiers tend to be weak, short-lived, and largely ineffective. Whether the same would hold for a similar effort on the part of the "new right," however, cannot be ascertained. Third, efforts on the part of some European military unions to initiate participative management by the military and the unions, at least in areas of responsibility where command prerogatives are not threatened, are likely to be replicated in this country in the event that military unions emerge. Finally, and perhaps most significant from the military perspective, the European armed forces which are unionized do not seem to be any the less effective.

These considerations notwithstanding, the differences between the traditions of the European and American union movements suggest that caution be exercised when drawing on the findings of a study of European military unions. A somewhat better analogy, perhaps, is that the American union movement could provide some insights into the shape that might be assumed by American military unions, and what they might be expected to do. In Chapter Seven, Professor Thomas C. Wyatt of the George Mason University of Virginia looks at these points from a sociological perspective in "American Military Unions." He finds that worker alienation is at least as important a stimulus to unionization as are economic incentives, and that the process by which military unions might form will affect the performance of whatever unions actually emerge. One of his more interesting conclusions is that, while military unions can be expected to form, it would be difficult to maintain them. This is because of the problems involved in identifying the true beneficiaries of union benefits *within* the services, and separating the roles of union leadership from roles of military leadership. To be both enduring and effective as a bargaining agent, the structure of the military union would have to be such that union leadership would not be identified with military management, *at least by the workers.*

Several implications of military unionization were summarized. First, since unions are powerful instruments of pressure for legislation favorable to its membership, some control over military legislation would be exercised by a military union. Second, combat effectiveness probably would not be impaired by unionization, *unless* the same individuals held leadership positions in both the union and the military chain of command. Third, union participation in the area of personnel management (e.g., promotion boards) would require a major readjustment to policy. Fourth, the potential for the politicization of unionized armed forces cannot be overlooked, even though this would be partisan (favoring the Democratic party) rather than ideological in character. Finally, the very process of unionization, successful or not, could polarize servicemen more explicitly, and in more enduring opposition, than heretofore has been the case.

It is obvious that there are points of agreement as well as disagreement among the preceding chapters. In Chapter Eight, entitled "Military Unionism in America: Retrospect and Prospect," I draw on the analyses that have been presented in this volume and elsewhere to provide a set of preliminary conclusions on the six issues in the debate on military unionization that were identified by Colonel Taylor in Chapter Two. The fundamental question concerns the consequences of military unionization for the functional effectiveness and political responsiveness of the American armed forces. After reassessing the relevance of American public sector unionism and Western European military unionism for the evolution of American military unions, it is concluded that military unions are simply too great a risk for a political democracy with global responsibilities and finite resources for its national defense. Blue-collar soldiers may be appropriate for states whose armies do not really expect to have to fight, at least if the unions involved are company unions. Otherwise, it is unwise to expect unions not to act like unions over the long term, and in so doing call into question the basis of our national security.

The question of military unionism is obviously an issue whose importance in the field of American national security policy is becoming increasingly apparent. It is also a challenge that must be dealt with soon if it is to be managed at all. The advent of blue-collar soldiers in the American armed forces would pose a number of constitutional, political, and military questions which would be likely to test this country's institutions of government and society to a greater degree than at any time since the Civil War. It is hoped that the analyses and arguments presented in this volume will facilitate the attainment of a better understanding of the character of military unions, and what they would mean for the United States.

Chapter Two
ISSUES IN MILITARY UNIONIZATION*

by William J. Taylor, Jr.

BACKGROUND FOR MILITARY UNIONIZATION

The concept of unionization of the "active duty" military in the United States is relatively new—an outgrowth of the all-volunteer system. The short-lived American Servicemen's Union (ASU), a manifestation of the antiwar movement in the United States of the late 1960s, was a real concern of the moment for the military leadership, but the ASU was never taken seriously as a "union movement." With the end of the Vietnam War and the demise of the conscription system, both the antiwar movement and the ASU disintegrated. However, there were a number of court cases growing out of antiwar protests which dealt with the First Amendment rights of free speech, assembly, and association. These cases have a bearing on the constitutionality of the right of servicemen to join unions and engage in union activities.

There are unions in the United States which have involved military reservists and members of the National Guard in union activities, for example, the Association of Civilian Technicians and the National Maritime Union. Some in the active duty military also are employed "off-duty" in nonmilitary jobs and hold union memberships in their nonmilitary capacity. All of these categories of union membership, however, are fundamentally different from membership by active duty military personnel in unions of public employees that purport to represent them in matters relating to their service in the armed forces through collective bargaining with agencies of the federal government. The difference is union representation

---

*The views and conclusions expressed herein are solely my own and do not represent the policy of any government agency of the United States. This essay was designed to establish debatable issues and, accordingly, to portray arguments for and against military unionization, and therefore I caution against selective reading or quotation out of context. I am grateful for the suggestions of several officers from the Department of Social Sciences and the Office of Military Leadership at the U.S. Military Academy who devoted their most scarce resource—"off-duty time"—to assist a professional colleague. Included are: Bill Wix, Roger Arango, Al Futernick, Jody Glore, Sandy Hallenbeck, Bob Lockwood, Hobie Pillsbury, Ken Carlson, Gary Moon, and Bill Sammon.

of the *collective* interests of active duty U.S. servicemen, as opposed to reliance upon military channels now open to military personnel individually and upon other channels open to several nongovernment organizations which purport to lobby on behalf of U.S. military personnel collectively.

Any serious attempt to unionize American active duty personnel must be viewed as a new phenomenon. It comes as a surprise to some that systematic union bargaining in the United States has a very short history indeed. Collective bargaining in the private sector received the protection of federal law only four decades ago with the enactment of the Wagner Act. Despite previous efforts, mass unionizing did not succeed until the movement of 1935-1945. The growth of public sector employment from the programs of the New Deal forward has been rapid. In the decade between 1965 and 1974 public sector employment increased 42 percent, whereas the increase in the nonargicultural private sector was only 26 percent. [1]

This rapid expansion of the public sector, it has been suggested, has led to an erosion of public authority. [2] This erosion has been manifested in many ways, one of which is the growth of public unions. In the late 1950s and 1960s, a series of successful constitutional attacks against the authority of states to abridge the First Amendment right of free speech, assembly, and "association" led to the right of state and local public employees to organize and join labor unions. The subsequent acceleration in the growth of unions of public employees has been impressive.

In early 1962, President John F. Kennedy issued Executive Order 10988, which established the basis for employee-management cooperation in the federal service. Among other provisions, the order recognized employee organizations as bargaining representatives, prohibited the unionization of "national security organizations" (specifically the CIA and FBI), limited the rights of employees to strike, and authorized advisory arbitration as the final step in a negotiated grievance procedure. Executive Orders 11491 (1969), 11616 (1971), and 11838 (1975) further clarified the rights of labor organizations and federal agency management.

It is important to note, however, that these excutive orders have not addressed the issue of membership by *military* personnel in public unions. None of the developments in the rights of public employees to join unions representing them in their principal job capacities touched on the rights of active duty servicemen to join and engage in union bargaining activities. The reason is that, for Americans, it has been "unthinkable" for servicemen to join in union activities which could place them in an adversary role vis-a-vis government authority.

Very recently, however, some have begun both thinking and doing something about the unthinkable. In September 1976, the delegates to the American Federation of Government Employees (AFGE) National Convention voted to amend the AFGE constitution, making armed forces personnel eligible for union membership. In early March 1977, the AFGE Executive Council voted 15-2 in favor of a plan for recruiting military members. As of mid-April 1977, the AFGE was polling its civilian members to guage the extent of support for signing up the military. AFGE President Kenneth Blaylock has stated that the results of the membership vote would be made public no later than October 1, 1977. He called "unionization of the military inevitable." [3]

SIX ISSUES

Inevitable or not, six basic issue-areas are involved in any consideration of American military unionism. All are not of equal importance, yet each must be taken into consideration.

Issue 1: Societal Trends and Public Employee Unions

Whether or not there are societal trends driving the nation toward military unionization is an issue of considerable importance. Social psychologists tell us that "there is an ideological movement afoot among the industrial, democratic nations of the Western world to enhance the 'quality of work life.' [4] This movement is referred to variously as "industrial democracy," " "codetermination," or "worker democracy." Trends in this direction are not new; their underpinning is the general historical shift in the Western world toward democratic and egalitarian principles. Made possible in large part by the trade union movement which preceded it, the movement has accelerated over the past ten to fifteen years, manifesting itself in growing employee preceptions of: (1) arbitrary treatment at the hands of management, and (2) discontent with dehumanized working conditions and meaningless work. [5]

The most fundamental aspect of the "youth revolution" of the late 1960s was a shift in approach to authority ("the establishment") in both its governmental and private sector managerial forms. Many have assumed that this more critical prespective would disappear with age and the assumption of responsibility for making a living wage. This assumption appears to have been incorrect. The new generation of employees ". . . will expect their immediate suprevisor to recognize their individual talents and to challenge these talents in an atmosphere that allows them as much freedom as possible to 'do their own thing.' " [6] The approach to organization itself has been changing:

Thus we find the emergence of a new kind of organization man—a man who, despite his many affiliations, remains basically uncommitted to any organization. He is willing to employ his skills and creative energies to solve problems with equipment provided by the organization, and within temporary groups established by it. But he does so only so long as the problems interest him. He is committed to his own career, his own self-fulfillment. [7]

There are many reasons (e.g., the education revolution and the information revolution) for such a widespread shift in mass psychology, all of which are too complex for treatment here. But the fact is that employees seem to have become more interested in personal dignity and "fate control" than they are in wages and benefits, even if one concludes that the latter requirements are being satisfied to such an extent that fulfillment of the former becomes predominant simply by default. The drive for personal dignity in the work environment manifests itself in many ways, one of which is the movement toward "codetermination," or worker participation in management decisions which both condition one's everyday life and shape the organizational mission. Thus, although primarily serving other human needs (pay, benefits, promotion, retirement, etc.), unions have become another medium for achieving fate control, especially but not exclusively in the private sector.

Unions of public employees have grown substantially over the past fifteen years. Between 1960 and 1970, for example, the number of federal employees with active memberships in the American Federation of Government Employees (AFGE) grew by 362 percent; membership in the American Federation of State, County, and Municipal Employees (AFSCME) grew by nearly 112 percent. By 1975 close to six million government employees were members of labor organizations. [8] The implications of this trend are important:

The growth of public employee unions has necessitated a major change in attitude on the part of legislators, the bureaucracy, and the public alike. Many public employees argue that they, like employees in private industry, have the right to join employee organizations that will represent their interests before boards of supervisors, city councils, school boards, and state legislatures. [9]

But the impact of this trend is far from certain:

It has frequently been argued that public employee unions will gain enough power through strikes to compromise government authority and the wishes of the people. But no factual confirmation of this is readily available, . . . Governments are not weak when challenged by unions and strike threats.
....
As a matter of practice, however, legislative bodies can no longer ignore public labor organizations. [10]

There does appear to be a societal trend in mass perceptions of the nature and conditions of employment, but its impact is a debatable issue. Clearly, a military establishment which draws its personnel from the larger society is not totally immune from the effects of such a trend.

Issue 2: Diverse Views on Unionization of the Military

We do not know very much about how different groups within our society view the notion of military personnel joining unions. Already, 72 percent of all army and air National Guard technicians are represented by a public employee union—the Association of Civilian Technicians—and have been engaged in collective bargaining. There has been very little publicity about this, and few realize that, in effect, military units have been involved in collective bargaining for quite some time. [11] A large but unknown number of active duty military personnel also are members of various unions by virtue of off-duty employment ("moonlighting").

One's view toward unions of military personnel would be shaped by a large number of factors. Philosophical predisposition, modified by such variables as age, educational level, and social and cultural backgrounds would be important. Whether one's occupational level is management or employee would count, as in the adage "where you stand depends upon where you sit." And, of course, there are many different forms of union activity prescribed or proscribed by law. Would a union representing military personnel have the right to strike, the right to bargain, or the right to lobby? There are, of course, enormous differences among the three, and one's view of military unions would be influenced significantly by what rights such unions might be accorded by law.

Views within the Armed Forces Ranks

The views of the target population for union membership, over 2 million active duty personnel and 700,000 members of the National Guard and reserves, are relatively unknown. Few surveys have been taken, and even fewer results have been released. A 1976 sample of 936 air force personnel, however, may be instructive. Forty percent of those surveyed said they would not join a military union; and 30 percent were undecided; but the remaining 30 percent stated that they would join a military union. Enlisted personnel were much more pro-union than were officers (37 percent versus 16 percent). An overwhelming majority of the sample (91 percent) responded that "military fringe benefits are being eroded, and 61 percent agreed that a military union could prevent that erosion." [12] But many believed that military unions would impact adversely on air force effectiveness (49 percent), military discipline (55 percent), and supervisor-subordinate relations (45 percent). Few within the ranks of the armed forces, of course, know much about unions or union practices. Whether or not these preliminary results would hold if the sample included large numbers of military personnel informed about the organization, functions, problems, and prospects of the public unions most likely to represent their interests cannot be prejudged.

To the extent that there exists "in the ranks" support of military unionization, there are related sets of explanations. The first of these appears to be partially a result of a previously discussed social-psychological trend toward preferences for industrial democracy and codetermination. Many young people, especially the better educated, do not feel an obligation for military service. [13] Many who join voluntarily are attracted principally by the offer of material benefits. [14] Many, again the better educated in particular, bring with them expectations concerning certain "human rights" and rights related to their working conditions and terms of employment.[15]

Some have argued that the end of military conscription and the creation of an all-volunteer force in the United States has fundamentally altered the principal motivation for people to join and remain in the armed services. As this argument goes, with the advent of the volunteer force, the traditional notion that young men have a patriotic duty (bound up in American symbolism and belief) to serve in the American forces has disappeared. [16] The "antiestablishment" sentiment, partially manifested in "antimilitarism," which developed as an offshoot of the antiwar movement of the Vietnam era, was partially responsible for this change. The end of conscription removed the legal presumption that eligible young males should serve in the armed forces. Finally, there has been an increasing lack of credibility in the need for large standing armed forces in an era of detente when threats to the security of the United States are not widely perceived. In brief, given alternative employment opportunities, young Americans would prefer "business as usual" to public service in the military. [17]

There is some evidence for this view in the rationale for a volunteer force set forth explicitly in the Gates Commission Report. [18] That report ". . . placed the primary reliance to recruit an enlisted force on monetary inducements determined by the prevailing marketplace economy, and thus emphasized the 'occupational' aspects of military duty." [19] Given a relatively healthy economy in the first three years of transition toward a volunteer force (1970-1973), the armed services found themselves in manpower competition with civilian industry. Military recruitment efforts focused on the creation of personal incentives—higher salaries, combat arms bonuses, educational opportunities, and military working and living conditions more commensurate with other walks of life. The more "sophisticated" recruitment advertising became (relying on industrial advertising models), the more

16

the notion of military service tended to become a job opportunity and less a patriotic obligation. This clearly has become a problem under the volunteer military system.

The all-volunteer force was proclaimed a reality by the secretary of defense in January 1973. Simultaneously, the inflation of 1973 began to take its toll on military personnel costs, which grew rapidly to constitute approximately 56 percent of the defense budget. Both critics of large military spending and congressional and defense budgeteers interested in holding the line on rapidly escalating military personnel expenditures sought ways of cutting costs. Many of the measures studied or adopted impacted upon military benefits. "Military entitlements" such as shopping privileges in post exchanges and commissaries at prices below the civilian retail market, free medical benefits for servicemen and women and their dependents, adjusted active duty pay scales for comparability (with civilian pay scales), educational opportunities, and adequate retirement pay have long been viewed by service personnel as implicit parts of the military contract. Increasingly, these entitlements have been attacked as "benefits" which are not in perpetuity and certainly not "contractual rights." [20] The result has been summarized succinctly by a former army vice chief of staff:

Members of the armed forces perceive a steady erosion in the benefits that were promised them in return for their services. This perception of neglect or breach of faith has resulted in a distrust of government by some of our uniformed personnel. Hence, they are turning to unions to represent them. [21]

The nature and extent of the alleged erosion of military pay and benefits, however, are not at all clear. The army chief of staff has noted recently a large number of areas in which established benefits have been defended successfully and new benefits approved, and Senator Sam Nunn recently has disputed claims of erosion of benefits. [22]

Another factor precipitating the fledgling movement to unionize service personnel is purportedly related to military working and living conditions. Despite the reforms implemented during the first years of the all-volunteer force, a reaction to such liberalized policies supposedly has occured in the military. [23] Efforts to hold the line against rising military personnel costs also have human costs. Manpower reductions without simultaneous reductions in functional requirements mean that fewer people have to do the same job. Sometimes greater efficiencies result; sometimes people simply have to work longer and longer hours for the same pay. "Holding the line" against inflationary increases in other budget categories has a severe impact on military living conditions, such as the construction and repair of military housing and the length of overseas tours of duty. The consequence, some have argued, is that the everyday facts of military life do not coincide with previous recruitment advertising. [24] "Grievances" growing out of such conditions are not readily resolved by the traditional military chain-of-command or the Inspector General system. Company, battalion, and brigade commanders have little impact on decisions concerning manpower levels and funding levels. They can attempt to explain to subordinates why conditions exist; they can exercise leadership to attempt changes in perceptions and motivations; but they cannot remove the direct causes of fundamental problems resulting from inadequate manning or funding. Whether real or imaginary, these two fundamental arguments—that there has been an erosion in both material and individual "rights," and that existing mechanisms for promoting "justice" for service personnel are inadequate—have laid a foundation of support for military unions. [25] How solid that foundation is remains to be determined.

Views of the Public at Large

Very little is known about public attitudes on military unions. One 1976 opinion survey, based on a sample of 1,529 people across the country, asked: "Do you favor or oppose members of the U.S. armed forces being organized into unions?" and "Do you believe members of the armed forces should be permitted to go on strike?" Eighty-two percent opposed military unions, although it should be noted that this may have been influenced by linking union membership with the strike issue. The strongest opposition to military unions came from those over forty-five years old, those with some education beyond high school, and those who are nonunion government employees. The greatest support for military unions came from those between eighteen and twenty-four years of age (33 percent) and from racial minorities (31 percent). [26] Media commentaries also tend to oppose military unions. [27] On the other hand a 1977 Defense Department contract study report concluded that traditional public apprehension concerning unionization of public safety services has largely dissipated and that "this is lowering the ultimate barrier to negotiations between military people and defense." [28]

View of the Commander in Chief

During a question and answer period following a March 1977 speech at the Pentagon, President Carter provided his views on recent efforts to organize the military under a union:

Well, my own opinion, which is strongly held, is that it would not be advisable to have the military personnel unionized. And I think my own public expressions might have a beneficial effect. The support that I would hope to engender among the American people for this position, combined with Congressional action if necessary, should be adequate. I don't know of any strong move in that direction and I believe that most of the leaders of our national and international labor unions are agreed. I've never had any of those leaders approach me with the intention of going forward with this effort. I know it has been discussed in isolated areas and by some responsible people. But, I think the national leaders in the labor movement have no commitment to this proposition.

Answering a follow-up question concerning legislation to prohibit military unions, the president stated:

I don't know how to answer that question. About constitutionality. I'm not a lawyer and I think that this—I don't know how to answer your question about specifics of legislation. I have no intention at this time to introduce legislation of that nature, and whether it would be constitutional, I don't know. [29]

He added that he did not feel that legislation to prohibit military unionization is necessary at this time.

Views of Defense Management

Nothing could be clearer than the public stance of the current civilian and military leadership in the Department of Defense—total opposition—although there is disagreement on how "the threat" should be handled. [30] Some, such as the assistant secretary of defense for manpower and reserve affairs, David P. Taylor, conclude for several reasons that military membership in unions would serve the interests of neither military personnel nor the public unions. [31] Other views are:

Secretary of Defense Harold Brown: "The functional role of our armed forces demands absolute certainty of immediate and total responsiveness to lawful orders. . . .Collective bargaining in the military is 'fundamentally incompatible' with the need for 'an unencumbered command and control system. . . .' " [32]

Secretary of the Army Clifford L. Alexander, Jr.: "There is no place for collective bargaining in the chain of command, and if the Army does its mission well, there will be no need for a union." [33]

Chairman of the Joint Chiefs of Staff General George S. Brown: "I think unionization and the operation of the military forces are totally incompatible." [34]

Army Chief of Staff General Bernard W. Rogers (in statement with former Army Secretary Martin R. Hoffman): "The Army has consistently maintained that military unions are totally incompatible with the chain of command and the need for military discipline." [35]

Similar opinions have been voiced in congressional testimony by senior military officers of the Air Force, Navy, and Marine Corps. [36] Most official statements focus on three central points:

1. Union representation of active duty military personnel would undermine the chain of command and erode military discipline.

2. Sound leadership and management obviate the need for union representation of armed forces personnel.

3. Congressional support for the fundamental needs of military personnel obviate any need for a union representation.

But at least one former official of the Department of Defense, former Assistant Navy Secretary Richard Beaumont, has been critical of the position toward military unionization taken by military management:

The military is fantastically naive about what individuals will suffer. . .the fact that the military has not organized earlier is one of the great perplexing phenomena as far as I am concerned. One of the major tasks is to prepare its leadership for the fact that they may organize. I don't think we have any perception of how we are going to manage the unionization of the military. The theory in the military is that if we don't talk about it, it will simply go away. [37]

Views of Military Associations

The active membership of these organizations tend to be senior active duty or retired commissioned and noncommisioned officers. In general, they represent rather traditional and conservative views philosophically at odds with the tenets and operational approaches of unions. There are twenty-two such associations, several of which have gone on record in strong opposition to military unionization. [38] Concerning the approach of the military associations and the American Legion, one noted observer has concluded:

It is difficult to read the protestations of the various special interest groups which have grown up among veterans without sensing the strong smell of sour grapes. In a sense they view the union as rebuke and possible threat to their own power and continued existence. [39]

Conversely, one might regard the military associations as representing the distilled wisdom of seasoned, retired soldiers and sailors whose experience in civil-military relations, and in military leadership and management, has spanned decades of peace and war.

Congressional Views

"The congressional view" that counts here is that of the potential majority voting to prohibit unionization of our military forces. A simple majority would suffice to head off those in the active duty military who might be inclined to join a public union. More would probably be required, however, to stop any public union bent on increasing its power through recruitment of military personnel. Such a union could and probably would challenge in the courts a statute prohibiting its recruitment of military personnel. This would be expected especially of a public union which had received a great deal of publicity concerning its intentions to unionize the military, and which had acquired sunk costs in its prestige vis-a-vis the public at large, the Congress it lobbies, the executive branch it lobbies and with which it negotiates and bargains, and with its parent union. One might suggest that by March 1977 the AFGE had placed itself in such a position.

The eventual position of Congress on this issue is unknown. In previous years, one might have anticipated overwhelming opposition to military unionization from older and more senior senators and representatives, many of whom were veterans of World War II or the Korean conflict, and some of whom could carry large voting blocs along with them. But the complexion of the Congress has changed in recent years with the advent of committee restructuring and the election of the "freshman Democrats" in 1974 (most of whom are no longer "freshmen"). In short, the Congress is less predictable on the issue than it might have been, say, prior to the Vietnam War.

Several bills to prohibit were introduced to the Ninety-fourth Congress; none got out of committee. By March 1977, nineteen new bills had been introduced to the Ninety-fifth Congress, eighteen of them in the House. [40] Probably the leading congressional opposition to military unionization in the past two years has come from Senator Strom Thurmond (S.C.), a fourth-term senator who served with the army in World War II, and later became a major general in the reserve and president of the Reserve Officers' Association. He is a member of the Armed Services, Judiciary, and Veterans Affairs committees. He introduced a Senate bill to prohibit military unionization in March 1976 (S. 3079). This bill had twenty-four cosponsors but Senator Thurmond was unable to schedule hearings because of the pressures of an election year, and the bill died. In January 1977, he introduced and referred another bill to prohibit military unionization to the Senate Committee on Armed Services (S. 274); this bill initially had thirty-three cosponsors. [41] Senator Thurmond has characterized the bill as follows: "This is not legislation against unions; it is legislation for a sound defense force for our nation." [42] Like its predecessor, this bill prohibited unionization of military forces, included criminal sanctions against uniformed personnel and civilians who attempt to organize the military into unions, and empowered the courts to fine any organization found guilty of such attempts. [43]

Although it is probable that relevant hearings will be held in both chambers of the Ninety-fifth Congress, one simply cannot predict how far the support for this or other bills to prohibit can be expanded in either the Senate or the House of Representatives. Should a bill make it to the floor, the size of the vote for it will be critical not only for passage but also for the survival in the courts of *any* statute prohibiting military unionization.

Union Views

As I have indicated earlier, there is growing interest by public unions in signing up the military. The Association of Civilian Technicians has already done so in the reserve and National Guard. The National Maritime Union has expressed an interest in organizing the military. The greatest interest at present, however, is found in the national headquarters of the American Federation of Government Employees. The view of the AFGE president is that organizing the uniformed military is not only feasible, but inevitable. The AFGE's National Executive Council Military Committee (NEC/MC) anticipates representation of the military in three areas: [44]

1. *Steward representation:* to encompass first-line grievance matter, excluding tactical operations, but including promotions, living conditions, and duty assignments. Subjects included are: housing, leave, foreign service, education and training, temporary additional duty, travel allowances, commissary and PX privileges, recreational facilities, parking, day care, dress and hair codes, political rights and their exercise, police, fire, and traffic regulations, health and dental care, efficiency ratings, promotions, EEO matters (womens' rights), safety, and reprimands or discipline under Article 15 of the Uniform Code of Military Justice (UCMJ).

2. *Legal representation as follows:*

Legal representation will be provided primarily in connection with administrative boards and uniform code of military justice proceedings. Discharge boards are of two basic types operating on "he could if he would but can't," and "he could if he wants but he won't" standards for discharge. There are also boards of inquiry and investigation, fitness for duty and correction of military records where representation may be required. UCMJ proceedings involve essentially military discipline under Article 15 UCMJ (so-called nonjudicial punishment) and summary special and general courts martial. Counsel appearing in serious cases, in special and general courts martial, are required to be certified to practice before the military courts. Two of our attorneys on the present legal staff possess these qualifications. It is highly specialized and we have numerous contacts in the specialized bar and foresee no problem retaining assistance as needed. Costs will be equivalent to our standard retainers under the legal rights fund.

3. *Legislative and policy representation,* including:

Pay–(through principally the Pay Council.) Thus this is derivative and is a provided service for which AFGE should claim appropriate credit.

Retirement–This is a *problem,* and policy positions must be worked out on 20-year versus 30-year military retirement, double dipping, service credits, and related benefits.

Benefits–This is another problem area for AFGE. Health care, insurance, commissary privileges, standby travel, etc., are under intense cost pressures.

The NEC/MC believes that union membership should be open to all active military service personnel, with the same rights, privileges, benefits, and dues as all other AFGE members.

Issue 3: Relevant Analogies [45]

In the growing numbers of public statements and written tracts about military unions, almost everyone uses analogies to the Western European experience. The analogies are used both by advocates and opponents of military unions, as well as those who advocate solutions short of unionization to the problems of the all-volunteer force.

Some advocates argue that, with some differences, the societal trend of industrial democracy now occurring in the United States is part of the broader movement originating in Western Europe. The growth of military unions in Western Europe is therefore instructive in the present American milieu. Since military unions have been "successful" in Western Europe, they can be so in the United States. [46] It is true that several Western European countries have military unions: Norway, Denmark, Sweden, the Netherlands, Belgium, Austria, and the Federal Republic of Germany. Most of the evidence available indicates that these unions have been more or less effective in achieving improvements in military prestige, working conditions, and compensation, comparable with similar improvements for employees in general. It is also correct that none of these unions has gone on strike, despite the confusion in the minds of some concerning the temporary "lockout" of the Swedish military by striking government officials in 1971. [47]

On the other hand, some opponents argue that there are fundamental differences between the Western European case and the situation of the United States—differences which render analogies irrelevant at best. First, there probably is not a valid "European model" for military unions. Such unions developed differently for various reasons in different Western European countries. [48] Second, most Western European countries with military unions also have conscription systems; the United States does not. Third, the trade union movements in Western Europe and in the United States are not at all analogous. For example, the governing Social Democratic parties in the Netherlands and (until 1976) in Sweden came to power largely because of the strength marshaled by trade unions. On the contrary, American unions have grown not only as adversaries to private management, but as political adversaries of federal, state, and local governments over those issues related to the rights of American labor. In the continental European case, where strikes by military unions are prohibited (except in Sweden), a military union "bargains" or consults with the elements of its own power base in government with which its interests are closely identified. In the American case, military unions would bargain in an adversary relationship with a government management whose political power base would rest upon a far more diverse span of interest.

The major "rights" enjoyed by unionized armed forces personnel in Western European countries are *not* rights secured by military unions through collective bargaining. In the main, they are rights secured by social legislation under social democratic governments in countries with strong socialist traditions. In Sweden, for example, the forty-hour work week was legislated   by the Social Democrats for *all* Swedish citizens, not simply as a collective bargaining agreement with one or more trade unions representing one or more of the Swedish military unions. The right of married couples in the Swedish military to decide whether the civilian working wife or the military husband will stay home to care for the newborn for the first six months is the legislated right of *all* Swedish couples whatever their work. Although it may appear ludicrous to many Americans that a soldier could simply inform his commanding officer, "My wife just had a baby; see you around in six months," the right to do so was important and "just" to the Swedish Parliament which passed such legislation. This line of argument, of course, does not suggest that European military unions do not serve well both thier constituencies and their societies. The point is that the societal context of such unions is simply different from the United States.

Other opponents argue or imply that unionized military establishments are undisciplined, referring to long hair, unkempt uniforms, lack of saluting, forty-hour work weeks, and other rights secured by military unions. Still others argue that "unions strike," an intolerable situation for the armed forces of the United States. Of course, these latter arguments (based on European analogies) are full of logical traps; one cannot have it both ways. For example, one cannot argue that unionized American military personnel would strike when the European analogies show that the unionized military do not strike. One cannot argue that where European military personnel have unionized, standards of appearance related to discipline have degenerated, for one might be forced in debate to extend the argument to prove conclusively (and causally) that mission capability has

24

degenerated. This would be a difficult and probably counterproductive undertaking.

Some, however, reject foreign analogies. Would unions involving active duty military personnel strike? There are no previous precedents to which one may turn, but there are sound analogies in the United States. Unions of public employees in the United States generally are prohibited from striking at both the federal and state levels. But the Postal Union struck in 1970 and was successful in having its demands met. [49] Police and firemen's unions are prohibited from striking in all fifty states, but many have done so, in effect, through work stoppages such as "sick outs" lasting as long as five days. [50] Clearly, strike prohibitions in executive orders or statutes do not serve as ironclad deterrents to strikes by strong unions of public employees. Can a union prevent its membership, or a part thereof, from striking? An AFGE president has stated:

There isn't any way to stop those things. They don't ask me to go on strike. They don't ask their national vice president to go on strike. . . .But the thing about it is that you cannot control individual elements of an organization whether it happens to be the United States Army as has been demonstrated a couple of times in the last three or four years, or the Navy or the Air Force or the AFGE. People take into their own hands what they think they have to. [51]

Finally, there are those who suggest that there are some analogies to some of the experiences of Western European military unions that *may* be useful in analyzing the situation in the United States, although care must be taken when doing so. [52]

Issue 4: Impact of Unions on Military Effectiveness

In order to project the impact of unions on military effectiveness, there are several preliminary considerations. First, one needs to assess who would join military unions, what organizational forms such unions might take, what form of recognition the unions might be accorded, and the scope of bargaining which would be involved.

Membership

Here one might look to two examples. First, to the extent that there are valid analogies, the European experience shows that any military member of *any rank* can join. Generally, however, conscripts are excluded. For example, in Sweden, there are three military unions for officers (SOF), warrant officers (KOF), and noncommissioned officers (POF). The POF and KOF are affiliated with the Central Organization of Salaried Employees (TCO). The SOF, on the other hand, is affiliated with the Central Organization of Swedish Professional Workers (SACO). These military unions have a long history. The KOF was founded in 1907, the POF in 1918, and the SOF in 1932. [53] The POF is most active and has by far the largest membership. Each union is represented at the national level by ombudsmen. For example, there are five ombudsmen for the SOF. Almost all (close to 100 percent) join thier respective unions as a matter of course. There is no great decision involved. Union activities are very low key; in fact, at the local level, it is very difficult to generate interest in attending meetings. For the SOF, monthly payments are 100 *krone*, which includes monthly dues, group insurance, and a special fund. [54]

The second example is the American Federation of Government Employees (AFGE) in the United States. An affiliate of the AFL-CIO, its active membership has declined from a high of 305,000 to 261,623, [55] but AFGE claims authorization to speak for "approximately 675,000 employees working in almost every department and agency of the United States Government, both home and abroad." [56] Its annual revenues averaged $7.3 million for 1974 and 1975. [57] Annual membership dues are $90 per person. The decision to join tends to be a relatively major one.

The AFGE represents professionals, technicians, clerks, administrators, and specialists in the classified white- and blue-collar career systems. The division between management and employee tends to differ among locals. In Washington-based Local 1812, which represents USIA personnel, including members under Foreign Service, Civil Service, and Wage System appointment authorities, there are 1,000 dues-paying members. This local has exclusive recognition for 2,000 employees located in Washington and overseas. The division between "management" and "members of the bargaining unit" is at a very high level. Overseas, only the ambassador and the deputy chief of mission are management. In the Department of State, the Agency for International Development, and the U.S. Information Agency, the assistant secretaries and counsels are management; deputy assistant secretaries or directors are in the bargaining unit. [58]

These two examples might suggest that, for U.S. military personnel in unions, all ranks could join, and the cutoff between management and members of the bargaining unit would be at the civilian assistant secretary of defense-assistant service secretary level. But it is indeed difficult to envision the Joint Chiefs of Staff accepting such a role, nor can one suggest readily what their roles would be. No one has come to grips with the knotty problem of drawing the line between "labor" and "management" were the military to be unionized. Asked precisely this question, the current AFGE president, Kenneth Blaylock, noted that there were no applicable rules and continued:

Where do you draw the line? You've got situations where you have colonels as technicians and you've got situations where a private first class is a fire-team leader—a supervisor. If you applied the same standards used to decide who's a manager with federal employees—the right to hire, fire, direct the work, make recommendations for promotions, you know—you run into trouble. You'd have to take them on an individual basis. If you take it on purely military and tactical structure, really anything above about E-4 would fall into management. But it's all conjecture. [59]

Organization

Organizing for military representation need not take the form of membership in public unions. The Foreign Service Association model is instructive here. This organization, which is about fifty years old and originated as a "club," is now a bargaining agent for foreign service personnel in the Department of State. This form of organization is not unique to the United States. The Federal Republic of Germany has a German Armed Forces Association which represents service members through the Trade Union of Public Service, Transport, and Traffic.

Were the U.S. military to organize an Armed Forces Association, it might resemble the old "company unions" which flourished after World War I as a counter to labor union attempts to organize employees.[60] One can envision alternative forms of amalgamation of the twenty-two existing private service associations in order to represent the interests of the armed services, rather than the individual services. However, large public unions with a known track record, such as the AFGE, will appeal for military personnel seeking short-term remedies to perceived problems.

Recognition

Military unions or associations, whether autonomous organizations or part of larger public unions, can have only the *legal* authority accorded to them by the government. Recognition could be informal, formal, or exclusive as was prescribed under Executive Order 10988. The first step toward gaining that authority is certification of "recognition." In order to acquire exclusive recognition, a public union must file a petition to represent employees of a government agency. To have the petition considered by the Department of Labor, the union must sign up at least 30 percent of the agency's members. Labor determines whether the bargaining unit and the agency have met the procedural requirements for a union election. If so, and if a majority of the agency's personnel vote for the bargaining unit, it receives recognition as the exclusive agent to represent all the employees in the unit where the election was held. Agency management and the bargaining unit representatives can then agree formally on the coverage and scope of procedures.

Scope of Bargaining

The central feature of this factor is that management attempts to limit the scope of bargaining through strict construction, whereas the union seeks to broaden the scope of negotiations. Since E.O. 10988, the scope of bargaining has broadened somewhat. The present prescribed scope can be found in E.O. 11491, as amended in 1975, the major features of which are:

1. Authorized bargaining representatives and management have the duty to meet and confer on personnel policies and working conditions, if appropriate. They are not required to agree on any issue, only to attempt in "good faith" to reach an agreement. [61] They can enter written agreements.

2. There are limitations on the duty to bargain in such areas as agency mission, budget, organization, and size and composition of work force.

3. The coverage and scope of grievance and arbitration procedures must be negotiated.

4. Dispute settlement is placed initially in the hands of the agency head.

5. Appellate authority rests with the Federal Labor Relations Council (FLRC).

6. Management prerogatives are nonnegotiable.

7. Wages and salaries are not included as permissible for bargaining.

8. The numbers, types, and grades of employee positions are excluded from bargaining obligation.

The scope of bargaining is further delineated by a growing body of case decisions by the FLRC.

Increasingly, the public unions have homed in on "inequities" in promotion and retirement policies and reduction-in-force (or "selecting out") procedures. Until 1971, there were no grievance or hearing procedures for the Foreign Service "selecting out" process. The AFGE obtained a legislative grievance board and a legal defense fund for the Foreign Service, obviating the need for lawyers' fees to correct personal injustices. And, increasingly, the AFGE has used the courts to provide due process. [62] Moreover, although public unions are not able to bargain over wages and salaries, they can lobby, and some have done so effectively.

The Right Vs. the Power to Strike

The possibility of a strike by a military union may be the most critical issue. As indicated above, all Western European military unions, except for Sweden, are prohibited from striking in the basic statutes which provide the right to unionize; none have struck. In the United States, public employee labor unions lack the legal *right* to strike, but they sometimes have the *power* to do so. Views are sharply divided on whether or not they should have the right, just as views were divided prior to the 1960s concerning whether public unions should have the right to bargain collectively with government management—a right now secured by public unions and protected by the courts. Those who argue against strikes in the public sector tend to rest their case on the sovereignty of government as rule maker [63], and on the "disruption of essential services which ultimately could bring government to a standstill." [64] Those on the other side of the argument advocate public employees' right to strike after "obligatory procedures" have been exhausted. [65] Other observers attempt to distinguish between "vital" services and those that merely "inconvenience" the public.

It appears clear that, whatever other rights military unions conceivably might be accorded in the United States, most would agree that the military provides a "vital" service. Some might be prepared to argue a distinction between missions in peacetime and in wartime, calling for a limited right to strike in peacetime—a right which would be vacated in times of national emergency. However, any who do so must come to grips with the peacetime mission of *deterrence* and the security implications of even short-duration strikes by military personnel. In any case, the record shows that unionized public employees will strike when they regard their work conditions as intolerable. "Clearly, by 1970, the strike was no longer the exceptional event in public sector labor relations" [66] at the federal, state, and local levels.

Impact Assessments

If one entertains the proposition that "Americans, in the military as in civilian life, attach the greatest importance to personal independence (controlling one's personal life and avoiding entangling bureaucracy) and to economic success (good pay and fringe benefits)" [67]; if one concurs with both defenders and critics of military unionism that the maintenance of a volunteer force has modified the perception of the nature of military service from a calling to a job [68]; if one concedes a growing awareness within the services that pay, benefits, and long-term security have been eroded by "arbitrary" management decisions; and if one understands that, at least temporarily, the law does not prohibit union membership by active duty military personnel, then, one can conclude that there is at least a possibility that a portion of the U.S. armed forces will become unionized.

What, then, are the potential advantages and disadvantages of military unionization? Any significant impact on unit morale, esprit, discipline, training, or readiness—all aspects of capability to accomplish the mission—yields advantages or disadvantages.

Advantages

Enhance Individual Sense of Security

Career military personnel and their families do perceive a significant erosion of those benefits that they assumed to be a part of an implicit contract on entering the service and on making periodic decisions about remaining in the military. How real and significant this erosion might be is not clear. However, widely read weekly service newspapers, such as the *Army, Navy,* and *Air Force Times,* carry numerous headlines of actual or pending reductions of medical, housing, educational, commissary, pay, and retirement benefits. These are subjects of frequent conversations among military families—conversations which reinforce perceptions of eroding benefits. It is also a belief among many military personnel—whether or not accurate—that no one is representing effectively the fundamental interests which impact heavily on their life styles. It is possible that public unions could fill this real or imaginary void, removing psychological insecurities, and, perhaps, stopping the actual erosion of benefits to the extent that it exists. There is empirical evidence that public unions have been successful in this regard. [69]

Enhance Personal Dignity

As indicated earlier, the drive for codetermination or "fate control" has become increasingly important to the personnel coming into the armed services. Immediate and unquestioned obedience to all lawful orders, a traditional expectation of military authority, is no longer in vogue. Military personnel want to know why given tasks should be done and wish to participate in decisions over their working conditions. With soldiers, as with most employees, persuasion (from the Greek *persuasio,* "through sweetness") elicits better sustained performance than edicts. It may also be the case that, if a boss cannot explain the necessity of performing certain tasks and spending long hours doing them, the jobs may in fact not be necessary.

The ideological movement toward codetermination involves an unwillingness to accept seemingly arbitrary decisions made somewhere, by someone, in an impersonal bureaucracy. For some in the military, the recent reductions in force have caused perceptions of arbitrary criteria applied in "selecting out" personnel, causing a major disruption, without due process, in the lives of those told to leave the service. If the AFGE experience with such matters serves as a model, it is conceivable that union representation in grievance procedures could serve to assure personal dignity. Given a requirement to negotiate in good faith with a union, commanders would be required, at a minimum, to consult with their subordinates on at least some applicable decisions.

Facilitate Communications

It is increasingly difficult for military leaders, especially at higher command and staff levels, to maintain the kinds of personal communications with their subordinates which have long been considered essential to sound leadership. The reasons for this are not complex. The numbers of reports required in an increasingly technical force structure and the numbers of tasks specified by higher headquarters have accelerated rapidly. These have grown in importance because, lacking frequent face-to-face observation, superior officers have been forced to rely on the quantitative indicators of subordinates' effectiveness contained in reports. The time available for leaders to meet with their subordinates—and to appreciate firsthand their hopes, fears, ideals, aspirations, and their problems—has been significantly curtailed.

Although the flow of military communications has always been two-way in theory, often the communications system has served primarily to transmit decisions by higher authority. The advent of junior officers and enlisted men's councils in the late 1960s theoretically could reinforce two-way communications. In the absence of the legal authority of organized unions, however, commanders always have the options of paternalistic disregard or co-option of these organizations. Military unions could prevent this from happening.

Improve Training and Unit Readiness

It must be noted that, if improved training and unit readiness were an unambiguous payoff from military unions, senior military officers themselves would probably opt for, support, and join unions *now*. But, like so many of the propositions subsumed by military unionization, this too is debatable. It is a fact that a significant problem commanders have confronted for many years stems from the requirements of "special duty" personnel. These are people assigned to the unit for a mission-specific job (e.g., tank gunner) who also are required to perform tasks unrelated to their jobs. There are so many examples: honor guard duty, brigade competitive sports teams, unit rifle and pistol marksmanship team, installation guards, club mess sergeants, and dozens of other "morale building" or "essential" duties. It is difficult (and often impossible) for commanders to conduct unit training with the entire unit, excepting perhaps large-scale maneuvers. Personnel detached for other jobs cannot be expected to return to their units in an emergency prepared to perform their principal assigned task—and everyone knows this. One major aspect of the union movement is to focus on the performance of well-defined tasks by specific individuals. The union requirement is generally that individuals be given work commensurate with a specific job description. Military personnel generally have had sufficient maturity to recognize job-*un*related tasks which detract from individual job proficiency and unit readiness. Meaningful work, enforced by the union, could underpin personal pride in proficiency and unit esprit. [70]

Attract Higher Quality Personnel to the Volunteer Force

Whether one likes it or not, the all-volunteer force is the status quo. Any recommendations worthy of adoption for "improvements" must be operative with comparative advantages, within the framework of the volunteer force. Although one wishes to avoid specifying the level of education at which it occurs, it is clear that the Western, secular, educational environment leads to a greater awareness of personal values, of one's role in and value to society, and to the drive to determine one's "fate." Thus, if public union representation of the military can achieve the previously discussed advantages, better educated, more highly motivated personnel will want to join and, perhaps, make a lasting commitment to the volunteer force.

Disadvantages

Strikes, Work Slowdowns, or Work Stoppages

This obviously will be a critical consideration for both advocates and opponents of military unions. The AFGE president was asked whether there would be a no-strike clause in the event the AFGE were to represent military personnel. He responded that "the AFGE constitution does not have a no-strike clause. We took that out many years ago. We'll be organizing the military under our constitution." [71] One cannot envision government agreement to an AFGE right to represent military personnel without a union agreement to stay on the job during both peacetime and periods of national emergency. However, "to date, little consideration has been given to no-strike clauses in federal labor-management agreements. . . ." [72]

As noted above, even without a *legal right* to strike, public unions representing large numbers of active duty military personnel will have the latent *power* to strike, as used by the Postal Service. Moreover, military personnel organized into a union will have the power to cause work stoppages such as "sick outs," or work slowdowns of a broad variety; police and firefighter unions have done so. Such operations would become public knowledge in short order. There is simply no doubt that such occurrences, if widespread, would be publicized or that they would cast doubt on the "readiness" (capability) of the U.S. forces to accomplish their assigned missions. Such doubts among potential opponents would undermine the credibility of the U.S. deterrent, both "conventional and nuclear."

Undermine Military Organizational Esprit

Unit esprit in the military is founded upon a number of esoterics—trust in, identity with, and dependence on the chain of command; individual and unit confidence in the ability to do assigned tasks well (in terms of job competence, physical stamina, and "just plain guts"); camaraderie, and the respect of others in other "professions." The first of these foundations, relating to the chain of command, at some point will be eroded. Now one does not want to make too much of this at levels above the army division. Unit esprit, built on pride in and loyalty to a unit, is "normally" (that is, in peacetime) a smaller unit phenomenon. This is not surprising in a democracy where one's allegience traditionally begins with the smaller corporate unit. True, Americans always have been motivated somewhat by *ideals*, especially in times of crisis, but Americans are not necessarily bound by an ideology. Wherever in the rank structure officers are identified as "management," the problem with unit esprit begins. It must not be forgotten that the union-management relationship approximates the zero-sum game; unions want a share of authority which has been a management prerogative, especially in the military hierarchical structure. What unions gain, management loses.

In discussions on the topic of military unionization, some of the better junior military commanders have stated that, in the advent of military unions, they might themselves join early because they would not want a wedge driven in the chain of command which would create a "we-they" relationship eroding unit esprit. This is, of course, a function of the definitional division between "management" and "the bargaining unit." The division might not occur between officers and enlisted personnel; it could occur between active duty military personnel and the civilian defense management. This leads to the most portentous disadvantage of all.

Derogation of Civilian Control of the Military

This could be construed to be a major danger of unionization of the military. The traditional concept of civilian supremacy has been thoroughly embedded in the professional ethos of career military personnel. [73]

The concept is implicit in the "chain of command," that is, what one requires of his subordinates one owes to his superiors. It has been nurtured by the sense of "national duty" or "calling" inherent in the demands of conscription which, admittedly by aberration in American history, was the norm for more than an entire generation from 1940 to 1973 (excluding an eighteen-month lapse in 1947-1948). Nowhere has the sovereignty of government been more manifest than in the accepted subordination of the military.

The alleged effects within the military of the societal trends suggested at the beginning of this essay have been extensively documented. [74] Civilian control, an externally oriented institutional norm based on benefit to the nation rather than the individual, could be eroded by the shift to occupational norms, which emphasize self-interest over service to the nation. The clearest manifestation of this development would be the organization of the military in a bargaining unit to achieve personal goals in conflict with institutional goals established by management—in this case elected civilian leadership and appointed, congressionally confirmed, civilian leadership. It is important to understand that the very nature of the bargaining relationship resides in a zero-sum game, "one in which union wants a part of the authority which management has or at least wants to exercise some influence over it." [75] Moreover, union membership by significant numbers of active duty military personnel undoubtedly would lead to greater political awareness and a more widespread perception of problems for which a united union front provides quickest solutions.

The military institution has enormous potential for intervention in politics—a virtual monopoly of the instruments of power, effective organization, and a sense of mission. The military as a corporate entity *en genre* is also relatively unique in its corporate self-interest. As one authority has explained:

The military is jealous of its corporate status and privileges. Anxiety to preserve its autonomy provides one of the most widespread and powerful of motives for intervention [in politics]. In its defensive form it can lead to military syndicalism—an insistence that the military and only the military is entitled to determine on such matters as recruitment training, numbers, and equipment. In its more aggressive form it can lead to the military demand to be the ultimate judge on all other matters affecting the armed forces.

....

. . . such claims are bound to bring the military into conflict with the civilian government which traditionally occupies itself with such matters. [76]

The extent to which the military today is alleged to perceive current problems may be without precedent. Certainly, the interwar period was one of extreme austerity for American armed forces. Yet there is a difference: the extent to which self-sacrifice to the ideals of professionalism or national calling may have been replaced by self-interest.

It is the aggregation of military interests under the auspices of a public union which may pose a threat to civilian control; and the threat should not be taken lightly. However, it is difficult to predict the nature of such a threat. On the one hand, a union which represents collectively the individual interests of military people may pose a range of problems requiring the attention of civilian defense management. On the other hand, it is not too difficult to envision a military union captured by an officer elite representing military institutional interests ranged against civilian leadership. It is the latter which poses the greater hypothetical threat to civilian control. The means of civilian control of the military potential to intervene is necessarily complex and ". . . if the ideal of civilian control is to remain viable, we need more than the bare provision of the Constitution in order to control what has clearly become the biggest institution in the world." [77]

Unacceptable Increases in Manpower Costs

In a sense, this disadvantage is related to the previous one. It is the intent of the civilian managers of the defense establishment to get a rein on soaring military personnel costs which now constitute 56 percent of the defense budget. Military views notwithstanding, this is clearly the prerogative of those who control military strategy and structure through policy-making, program management, appropriation, and authorization. Although some might suggest several alternative approaches to reducing military manpower costs, the choice of alternatives is an important aspect of civilian control. To the extent that a unionized military limits (through bargaining and, conceivably, union "actions") the range of choice of civilian decision-makers charged with defense management, civilian control is eroded.

Given the fact that a major stimulus toward military unionization is the perception that compensation and benefits are being eroded, there is little question that one of the top priorities of unions representing the military would be to roll back the attack on manpower costs. The leadership of the public union with the most active profile fostering military unionization, the AFGE, has referred repeatedly to the manpower cost issue. Either "stopping the erosion of benefits" [78] or "military pay comparability" [79] with the private sector is usually stated first among priorities. Assuming the continuation of a volunteer force of approximately the present size, 2.1 million people in uniform, union representation of the military in bargaining over benefits and pay will be a zero-sum game over manpower costs. To the extent that the union prevails in bargaining and lobbying, manpower costs will rise in real terms. Unless Congress is willing to raise defense budget ceilings in real terms, other defense programs will have to be cut, for example, funds earmarked for weapons development and production or for strategic mobility.

Issue 5: Constitutional Rights and Military Membership in Unions [80]

The central constitutional question concerning the right of active duty service personnel, in their principal duty capacities, to join unions centers on the First Amendment to the Constitution which prohibits Congress from enacting legislation abridging the rights of free speech, free press, and the rights to assemble and petition. The U.S. Supreme Court has held that the First Amendment constitutes the cornerstone of the American democratic system of government and has found inherent in the First Amendment a "freedom of association." [81] Lower courts have held that public employees have a constitutional right to join labor unions under their First Amendment right to freedom of association. [82] In 1967, the Supreme Court held that Congress cannot pass laws under its "enumerated powers" if those laws place an excessive burden on the freedom of association rights of federal employees. [83] Thus, both Court decisions and the practices of the late 1960s support the right of public employees—federal, state, and local—to join unions and the unconstitutionality of congressional attempts to abridge that right. Although this precedent speaks to a wide range of public employees, some of whom might be termed "paramilitary" (i.e., police and firemen), it does not deal specifically with the case of the military.

The Supreme Court has consistently avoided entering the realm of authority and rights in the military, deferring to the Congress. The fundamental grant of congressional authority over the military derives from the Constitution:

Congress shall have the power. . . to raise and support armies, but no appropriation of money to that use shall be for a longer term than two years; to provide and maintain a navy; to make rules for the government and regulation of the land and naval forces. [84]

Two cases, one in 1953 and a second in 1974, contained the essence of the Court's consistent approach to the law applicable to the military and to the First Amendment rights of service personnel. In the first case, the Supreme Court dismissed a habeas corpus petition for two air force men convicted of rape-murder in Guam, finding:

Military law, like state law, is a jurisprudence which exists separate and apart from the law which governs in our federal judicial establishment. This court has played no role in its development; we have exerted no supervisory power of the courts which enforce it; the rights of the men in the armed forces must be conditioned to meet certain overriding demands of discipline and duty, and the civil courts are not the agencies which must determine the precise balance to be struck in this adjustment. The Framers expressly entrusted that task to Congress. [85]

In the second case, involving an appeal from a conviction of violating Articles 133 and 134 of the Uniform Code of Military Justice, the Court observed:

While the members of the military are not excluded from the protection granted by the First Amendment, the different character of the military community and of the military mission requires a different application of those protections. The fundamental necessity for obedience, and the consequent necessity for imposition of discipline, may render permissible within the military that which would be constitutionally impermissible outside it. [86]

Thus, where the military has had jurisdiction over an individual, the Supreme Court has refused to interfere with the military courts exercising a grant of authority from Congress to safeguard the rights of service personnel. The congressional grant of authority to military courts is found in the UCMJ enacted by Congress in 1950 and revised periodically since that time. The UCMJ establishes the framework for criminal jurisdiction and a system for appeals. The Supreme Court, on appeal, indicates that the First Amendment rights of armed forces personnel might be restrained where a deterioration of discipline impacts adversely upon a higher interest. Whether or not union membership would erode military discipline is clearly a critical issue.

One must note at this juncture that the Supreme Court has not spoken to the issue of military unions, deferring to Congress on the relevant First Amendment rights of military personnel, and Congress has not passed laws relating to unions of military personnel. Thus, one is forced to look elsewhere for legal guidance on the right to trade union membership for military personnel—to legal precedents from lower civilian courts and military tribunals. It is important to keep in mind that the First Amendment itself prohibits Congress from enacting legislation which abridges the rights of free speech, free press, the right to assemble and to petition, and, by Supreme Court extension, of freedom of association. The First Amendment applies to all American citizens. The central question is the degree to which any branch of government—federal, state, or local—can restrict military personnel from full exercise of the First Amendment rights which would form the basis of legal union membership by active duty military personnel in their principal duty capacities.

Court Decisions and Military First Amendment Rights

Military Court Decisions

The Court of Military Appeals has had several opportunities to address some of the issues concerning the First Amendment rights of military personnel. Representative of this Court's approach is a 1954 decision in *U.S.* v. *Voorhees,* involving an army officer's refusal to delete certain references in an article he was to publish. The Court's decision had three separate opinions. Each of the opinions agreed, grudgingly, that the protections of the First Amendment applied to military personnel. However, Judge Quinn's opinion referred to First Amendment rights as restricted by "military necessity." Judge Latimer elaborated on those restrictions:

I believe it ill-advised and unwise to apply the civilian concepts of freedom of speech and press to the military service unless they are compressed within limits so narrow they become almost unrecognizable. Undoubtedly, we should not deny to servicemen any right that can be given reasonably. But in measuring reasonableness, we should bear in mind that military units have one major purpose justifying their existence: to prepare themselves for war and to wage it successfully. Embraced in success is sacrifice of life and personal liberties; secrecy of plans and movement of personnel; security; discipline and morale; and the faith of the public in the officers and men and the cause they represent. In connection with this litigation, it is to be remembered that while we can discuss the principles involved in a time of temporary peace, that is the period during which we must prepare for war or other eventualities. A principle which interferes with preparing for war may interfere with its successful prosecution; and a privilege given unwittingly in peace may be a death knell in war. [87]

This and subsequent cases decided by the Court of Military Appeals establish a rather consistent approach to the First Amendment rights of military personnel. Military personnel have such rights, but they must be balanced by the unique requirements of "military necessity," loosely defined as requirements of military good order and discipline required for national security.

Civilian Courts

Although not addressing the issue of freedom of association, lower federal courts have ruled on First Amendment rights for military personnel in a number of cases which grew out of the Vietnam War protest movement. Representative is a 1969 decision in *Dash* v. *Commanding General, Fort Jackson, South Carolina.* Here a district court examined the authority of the post commander to restrict distribution of publications on post and to refuse a request to hold on post an open meeting to discuss the Vietnam War. The court first addressed the right of federal courts to decide such questions, holding that:

. . . however hesitant they may be to "intrude," courts will be available to determine whether there is a reasonable basis for such restrictions as may be placed on the servicemen's right of free speech by the military establishment. [88]

As to the basic issues, the court stated:

. . . in those cases where there is a reasonable basis for the conclusion that the distribution (of published materials) represents a "clear danger to the loyalty, discipline or morale of his troops" [the post commander may] prohibit the distribution. . . .

Can training for participation in a war be carried on simultaneously with lectures on the immorality or injustice of such war? In my opinion, the denial of the right for open public meetings at advertised meetings (sic) on post for discussion of the propriety of the political decision to participate in the Vietnam War was justified "by reason of the peculiar circumstances of the military" and represented no infringement of the constitutional rights of the plaintiffs or others similarly situated. [89]

Like the military courts, civilian courts have been relatively consistent in restricting the First Amendment rights of military personnel where the exercise of those rights was prejudicial to military good order and discipline or accomplishment of assigned military missions. The requirements of military necessity are to be balanced against the First Amendment rights of military personnel.

As of this writing, it appears that the courts at all levels will be forced to come to grips with the constitutionality of union-sponsored legislation concerning forced unionism in the public sector at the state, county, and local levels. [90] Thus, unionization in the public sector will remain a live issue. The specific question is how the courts will approach the rights of military personnel to join public unions and to exercise the rights of union members. It is important to note in this regard that the link between the prevailing political climate and court decisions is important. Most leading scholars of the American court system concur that the legal subculture in the United States increasingly reflects the societal power structure and that judges are not immune to its influence. [91] The potential impact—economic, social, political, and military—of court decisions on unions of military personnel and their rights to bargain would be enormous. How legislatures approach the matter will be important. Courts probably would be loath to nullify a broadly supported statute which either supports or prohibits anything which has such important implications for national security.

Issue 6: Alternatives to Military Unionization

It is possible that it is already too late to prevent military unionization. Two years ago it was apparent that the conditions under which people organize in unions had been established in the American armed forces. These included:

a. increasing unwillingness to accept seemingly arbitrary decisions of an impersonal and amorphous bureaucracy;

b. growing perception of inequity in working conditions, compensation, and benefits; and

c. heightened awareness that organization in a public union could provide an alternative to the dilemma of either suffering inequities in one's chosen employment, or prematurely terminating that employment, involving various "sunk costs."

The official position of the defense establishment, evolved from public statements and other reported comments by high-ranking members of the Department of Defense, has been that armed forces personnel may join unions, but commanders may not bargain with any unions which purport to represent those personnel. DOD officials generally have argued that military unions are bad because: unions undermine discipline, unions strike, unions of soldiers are unnecessary because the underlying problems giving rise to military unions are not severe and can be solved by sound leadership. Operationally, the early official position appears to have been to support congressional action to prohibit military unions and, otherwise, to refrain from official activity which might provide publicity for any movement to unionize the military. [92] No one should doubt that the best minds in defense management will remain abreast of the issues involved.

One thing is very clear. Union advocates notwithstanding, military unionization is not inevitable. The issues are political, and politics remains the art of the possible. First, as noted earlier, even court deliberations over the constitutionality of a statute to prohibit would not be free of important political considerations. Second, the creation of military unions with few active duty military members would be a relatively sterile undertaking. And third, unforeseen events such as a time of protracted national emergency could alter significantly the nature of the environment in which the movement to unionize the military has been incubating. In brief, there may indeed be time to design and implement alternatives to military unionization. However, the first step in solving a problem is to recognize that it exists. No one should think the solution will be easy. Former Secretary of Defense Donald Rumsfeld, in a reference to the utility of military unions, was correct in referring to H.L. Mencken's famous dictum "For every knotty problem there is a solution—neat, simple, and wrong." What then are the general shapes of some alternatives which might be complex, difficult, and right?

Reassurance through Leadership

Here one assumes the continuation of the volunteer force. The leadership is needed at two levels. The first level is the "corporate" leadership found at the highest level of each military service and in the Joint Chiefs of Staff. The second level is the "line" leadership found in the operational chain of command which, below the levels of the commander in chief, the secretary of defense, the unified and specified command commanders and their subordinate commanders, is the leadership impacting on soldiers, sailors, air personnel, and marines in their everyday working and living conditions.

Reassurance which can flow from the first level of leadership would be based on concerted action to halt a perceived assault on military compensation and benefits. No informed observer would even suggest that the service secretaries, service chiefs, and Joint Chiefs of Staff have not been making the case for manpower requirements to sustain a quality volunteer force. In fact, the result of recent efforts to reduce compensation and benefits assuredly would have been more severe had it not been for the representations of the service leadership. However, these representations do not appear to have stemmed growing unease in the active duty military. [93]

Subordination of the military to civilian control, a cherished tradition in the professional military as well as in American society at large, does not diminish the necessity of military "advice" in all its variants within a democratic system. Not only does military leadership have the right to present a strong case over major national security issues, it also has the responsibility to do so. Surveys indicate that the American public's respect for military leadership is high. [94] The public probably will expect a strong military stance over a national security issue as important as the manpower quality of the armed forces of the United States. History is replete with examples of military leaders who have staked their reputations and careers on strong positions at odds with the opinion prevailing in some quarters of government. Some of these professional soldiers carried the day [95]; some did not, with attendant personal sacrifice. [96]

The second level of leadership is clearest at the level of division commanders and below. These leaders have little or no influence over pay, benefits, funds for military housing construction and repair, the length of overseas tours, promotion and retirement policies, and so forth—unless one assumes that sound leadership is found at this level in the ability of a leader to explain to subordinates the reasons for erosion of benefits and get them to accept the status quo. However, it is largely within the capabilities of this level to influence the working and, to a somewhat lesser extent, the living conditions of service personnel. Effective leadership here can ensure that military service is the self-satisfying, self-fulfilling, and adventurous ("fun") experience which peacetime service can be. There are two paramount means of effective leadership in this respect. The first is sound "management by objectives," or establishing time requirements, resource levels, and standards for people in organizations and allowing them to determine their own methods for accomplishing objectives. The second means is "persuasion." General Dwight D. Eisenhower defined leadership as "the ability to get some-one to do something you want done because he wants to do it." The day of the "military martinet" is over, probably in combat as well as in peace-time garrison operations. Army General Donald V. Bennett once analogized authoritarian leadership as "like a bulldozer, it gets the job done, but leaves a great deal of wreckage in its path." In military organizations, the wreckage is people. In a voluntary military establishment, especially in times of low unemployment, people who have talents which are alternatively marketable (precisely the people one wants to remain in the service) will not tolerate arbitrary treatment; they will leave the service. Even worse, they will carry home to potential volunteers messages highly counterproductive to military recruitment.

Sound management by objectives is difficult in a defense establish-ment where manpower has been reduced from 3.5 million in 1970 to 2.1 million in 1977, but where the operational requirements appear to have remained constant or increased. It takes a talented and confident leader to tell his superiors why assigned objectives are unreasonable, given the resources and time available, and why the demands on his subordinate per-sonnel are excessive. It is much easier, in the short run, to say "can do, sir" and accept the attendant sacrifices the organization must make. In the long run, however, such an approach will clash with codetermination and worker democracy, forcing talented human beings to seek alternatives. Among these alternatives may be military unions or resignation, or both.

Reduction in Size of the Volunteer Force

Other things being equal, it is clear that rising manpower costs can be checked or even driven down by reducing the size of the military establishment. It is easy to demonstrate that, with the present force level and present management of programs for a volunteer force, manpower costs will continue to escalate. Although difficult, one can find areas where greater "efficiencies" can hold down somewhat rising manpower costs. In tandem with gradual personnel reductions, this is the present approach. However, large-scale personnel reductions can reduce manpower costs more rapidly. It is much more difficult to prove the case for maintaining the number of personnel and military units that we have. Debate theory and practice notwithstanding, military managers and strategists bear a heavy burden of proof in defending the existing force size. For example, against arguments based upon the increasing Soviet conventional military capability, critics of defense spending might argue Soviet lack of intentions to employ conventional forces against Western Europe, and that a lower manpower level linked to U.S. nuclear capability can serve as an adequate deterrent. Against arguments that a certain force level is required to perform essential military tasks, critics might argue that many of those tasks can be performed by civilians. Although one might conclude that defense management has defended its cases very well indeed, some suggest that the net result has been diminishing manpower levels and, much more noticeably, erosion of pay and benefits. Of course, another measure of the efficacy of defense management in this respect is the fact that, unlike most other postwar periods, America's armed forces have not gone through a period of rapid dismantling.

In any case, if the principal objective is to overcome current volunteer force problems leading to military unionization, a smaller force with pay and benefits intact would be a viable alternative. But there is no guarantee that this will stop the attack on manpower costs, even though such costs are lower. This also leaves out the critical question of national security capabilities at lower force levels.

Functional Equivalents of Military Unions

This approach could address only part of the set of problems behind the movement toward military unionization, and would exclude the issues of military pay and benefits. It is at least conceivable that in such areas as working conditions, some aspects of living conditions, promotion policies, policies and procedures for "selecting out," assignment policies, policies on punishment and awards, and grievance procedures, "bargaining units" might be established within the military. At the highest level of generalization, it is conceivable that enlisted personnel, noncommissioned officers, warrant officers, and commissioned officers as separate groups might be granted under law "associations" and procedures for representing their interests within the chain of command. Commanders might be required to establish grievance procedures which, under certain conditions, permitted circumventing levels of command, to negotiate certain other issues in good faith and, where appropriate, to enter bargaining agreements with elected representatives of the various associations. A functional equivalent of the Foreign

Service Grievance Board, but comprised of both civilian and military officials, might be established as an organization for final appeals. [97]

If legalized and regularized, these procedures might remove the traditional inhibitions of individuals to take their grievances or seek representation of their interests through the chain of command or through the Inspector General system which some view as an extension of command authority. Group representation of interests might serve also to prevent command "retribution" in unjustified circumstances. Although undoubtedly difficult to establish, this system could serve to enhance personal dignity and serve the needs of codetermination. Commanders could choose to join the officers' association or not; either way, they would have to confront collective representation procedures. They might, however, be well advised to join as a means of understanding better the functioning of the system and the nature of the association. Would such a system undercut command authority? One is predisposed to judge that judicious command authority would be enhanced and that arbitrary command authority would confront formidable difficulty. A premium might be placed on *how* a commander accomplishes objectives, as a measure of *whether* he accomplishes them.

Compulsory National Service

Very recently, there has arisen interest in either reviving the draft or in universal national service. Advocates of these approaches tend to base their cases on problems with the volunteer force including: (1) soaring manpower costs, (2) falling unemployment and implications for volunteers for military service, (3) racial imbalances in the armed forces, and (4) the shrinking manpower pool. [98]

Those opposed to such schemes tend to argue that: (1) the volunteer force is working, (2) a draft would result in insignificant manpower costs savings, (3) manpower problems can be solved by recruiting more women, (4) military manpower costs are acceptable for an effective fighting force, (5) new policies suited to a volunteer force should be adopted, (6) physical standards for noncombatant jobs should be lowered, thereby releasing more men for combat units, and (7) the present system should be made more efficient. Except for the fifth argument, the analysis for which has yet to be elaborated publicly, none addresses the societal trends toward codetermination and worker democracy. It is doubtful that increased military pay levels within the range of feasibility could compensate for perceived usurpation of fate control by an arbitrary bureaucracy. It is almost certain, given the equal rights movement, that women *will not* find tolerable the working and living conditions with which men have expressed dissatisfaction. One cannot imagine that males with lower physical capabilities would be more satisfied than others with conditons of the volunteer force. And, of course, the drive for "greater efficiencies" in the volunteer force already has been a catalyst in a preception of erosion of pay and benefits. Thus, some form of national service, either voluntary or compulsory, or a combination of both, may be the best alternative to military organization under public service unions.

One such concept was recently advanced by the sociologists Morris Janowitz and Charles C. Moskos, Jr. These noted scholars approach their proposal with a preliminary rejection of two alternatives. First, they rule out return to the draft:

... the goal of reinstituting the draft might well result in troop morale and discipline problems exceeding what the military system could accommodate to. In fact, mass conscription does not meet the manpower needs to a military force 'in being' designed for global deterrence. [99]

Second, they dismiss compulsory national service schemes because they "would likely be construed as 'involuntary servitude' within the meaning of the Thirteenth Amendment and thereby be ruled unconstitutional." [100]

Moskos and Janowitz advocate a two-year "voluntary national service program—in which military service is one of several options—which would be a prerequisite for future federal employment." [101] The main features of the program would be:

1.   service, after high school, during college, or after college;
2.   compensation at levels comparable to the former draft;
3.   inducement based largely on post-service educational benefits;
4.   appeal based on tasks for which monetary incentives intrinsically are not suitable;
5.   future eligibility for government employment based on completion of national service.

There are potential criticisms of such a scheme, but these are certainly premature, pending elaboration of the authors' initiative.

Another variation might be compulsory universal national service based upon a national lottery for people between specified ages from which there would be almost no exemptions. Exemptions would have to be medically certified and carefully monitored. However, there might be categories of exclusion from service in combat arms for people whose names would be included in the draws for all other forms of national service. Women might be so excluded based upon current policies. Those whose physical conditions might be inappropriate for combat arms would be included in all but combat arms lotteries. Similarly, those whose mental aptitude might be below standards for various forms of national service would be excluded from those, but they would be drawn to perform other appropriate tasks. With further refinement of a system of exclusions to match individual capability with task requirements, even the handicapped might not be exempted from compulsory national service.

Pay for various terms of service probably could not be rolled back from present levels, but it could be held there for some time. Present benefits which serve as inducements for voluntary military service, especially for combat arms, could be curtailed sharply. However, the level of pay and benefits established for compulsory service should be spelled out in contracts irrevocable except on clearly established grounds of *rebus sic stantibus*. Manpower costs therefore could be reduced sharply over a relatively short period. Over time, the view of military service as just another job (the occupational model) could be rolled back and the sense of national service restored as a "calling."

It would be important that the priority of this program remain the maintenance of a well-trained force in being for the primary purpose of conventional force *deterrence,* not the creation of a mobilization base of trained military personnel. During the great debates on universal military training in 1951, General George C. Marshall, an ardent advocate of UMT, stated the rationale for such a program:

In the event of a major war, the United States will be able to mobilize its combat strength within a considerably shorter time than heretofore. The reserve will no longer be perpetually understrength or inadequately trained. [102]

Marshall saw UMT as "the only alternative to the maintenance of large, burdensome, and potentially dangerous regular armed forces." [103] Marshall's view might have been appropriate for 1951 when, despite the Soviet A-bomb explosion of 1949, the United States enjoyed monopoly of strategic atomic capability. The United States still had time for mobilization in those days. Today, however, despite the problems and traditional fears of large standing armed forces, only such forces can serve the principal security task of strategic deterrence. Thus, despite all other benefits which might accrue from universal national service, the principal objective must remain the maintenance of a well-trained, immediately deployable, strategic conventional force. Obviously, this, as other alternative schemes for national service, is not beyond criticism. For example, the cost of managing such a program would probably be very high. And to the extent that high educational criteria were established, the military might become less a vehicle for upward social mobility.

Would the American public and the Congress be amenable to

proposals for universal national service? Although there is little evidence concerning public attitudes on *compulsory* national service, a recent Gallup Poll found that "two out of every three Americans favor a law requiring all young men to devote a year to national service either in the military or in nonmilitary work such as the Peace Corps of VISTA." [104] The same survey, however, showed that only 47 percent of young men of draft age (eighteen to twenty-four) would support such a scheme, and a majority of them indicated that they would opt for social work rather than military service. [105] Any proposal for universal national service must have strong support in Congress. In 1952, 70 percent of the public and the administration were in favor of UMT. Nevertheless, the House of Representatives rejected it and UMT was stillborn. [106] Thus, it appears that a *compulsory* national service program (CNS) might be the only viable alternative for *both* solving the problems of the volunteer force and for obviating the rationale for military unionization. Thus far, the two topics have been treated separately. The time has arrived for analysis of the two in tandem, for each has important implications for the nation's security interests. [107]

CONCLUSION

To the extent that there is a significant movement toward military unionization, the reasons for it are found in general societal trends and in the state of the volunteer force under the present national economy. Understanding the complexities of such a movement and planning for its impact demand interdisciplinary analysis. Military unionization could take any number of forms. Military unions are not "inevitable"; neither can they be "wished away." In politics there are always alternatives. Careful analysis and reasoned public debate can yield those alternatives.

NOTES

1. See Robert S. Lockwood, "The Costs of Military Strikes" (Paper prepared for presentation to the Military Operations Research Society Thirty-ninth Annual Symposium, United States Naval Academy, Annapolis, Md., June 28-30, 1977).

2. See Samuel P. Huntington, "The Democratic Distemper," *The Public Interest,* No. 41 (Fall 1975), pp. 9-11.

3. See *Newburgh* (New York) *Evening News,* 9 March 1977, p. 8, and *U.S. News and World Report,* 28 March 1977, p. 52.

4. Lauri A. Broedling, "Industrial Democracy and the future Management of the United States Armed Forces" (Paper presented at the Annual Convention of the International Studies Association, St. Louis, Mo., March 16-20, 1977), p. 1.

5. See ibid, pp. 2-4, and David G. Bowers, "Work Related Attitudes of Military Personnel," in Nancy L. Goldman and David R. Segal, eds., *The Social Psychology of Military Service* (Beverly Hills: Sage Publications, 1976), pp. 91-99.

6. Eugene Koprowski, "The Generation Gap, From Both Sides Now," in Gordon L. Lippitt, Leslie E. This, and Robert G. Bidwell, Jr., eds., *Optimizing Human Resources: Readings in Individual and Organization Development* (Reading, Mass.: Addison-Wesley, 1971), pp. 287-88.

7. Alvin Toffler, *Future Shock* (New York: Random House, 1970), p. 149.

8. See Edwin F. Beal, Edward D. Wickersham, and Philip K. Krenast, *The Practice of Collective Bargaining,* 5th ed. (Homewood, Ill.: Richard D. Irwin, 1976), p. 450.

9. Carl E. Lutrin and Allen K. Settle, *American Public Administration* (Palo Alto, Calif.: Mayfield Publishing Co., 1976), p. 208.

10. Ibid.

11. See Ezra S. Krendel and Bernard L. Samoff, eds., *Unionizing the Armed Forces* (Philadelphia: University of Pennsylvania Press, 1977), pp. 5-9.

12. See *Federal News,* 28 February 1977, p. 5.

13. See Ronald Inglehart, "Changing Values and Attitudes toward Military Service among the American Public" in Goldman and Segal, *Social Psychology,* pp. 274-77.

14. See David G. Bowers, "Work-Related Attitudes of Military Personnel," in Goldman and Segal, *Social Psychology,* pp. 92-97.

15. Ibid., pp. 111-14.

16. See, for example, David Cortright, "The Union Wants to Join You," *The Nation,* 21 February 1976, pp. 206-9; see also Tod Ensign and Michael Uhl, "Soldiers as Workers," *The Progressive* (April 1976), p. 37.

17. See the AFGE arguments cited by Gary R. Ballard, "Big Labor Pushing for Unionization of Armed Services," *Human Events Magazine,* 8 November 1975, p. 8. Charles C. Moskos, Jr., has alluded to the possibilities for such attitudinal changes; see his "Social Control of the Military" (Paper presented at the meeting of the American Sociological Association in San Francisco, Calif., on August 25-29, 1975), pp. 10-12.

18. See *The Report of the President's Commission on an All-Volunteer Force* (New York: Macmillan, 1970).

19. Charles C. Moskos, Jr., and Morris Janowitz, "Volunteer National Service: A Prerequisite for Federal Employment," mimeo. dated February 1977, p. 3.

20. See Major General Herbert C. Sparrow, USA (Ret.), "The Promises Men Live By," *Armed Forces Journal International* 112, no.9 (May 1975), pp. 21-22.

21. See General Bruce Palmer, Jr., Forword to "Unions in the Military," *AEI Defense*

48

Review (American Enterprise Institute for Public Policy Research), no.1 (February 1977), p. 1; see also Lieutenant John E. Kane et. al., "Is Military Unionization an Idea Whose Time Has Come?" *U.S. Naval Institute Proceedings* (November 1976), pp. 40-42.

22. See *Army Times,* 28 March 1977, pp. 1, 18.

23. See, for example, Colonel Richard M. Jennings, USA (Ret.), "The Military and Social Adaptation," *Strategic Survey* 4 no. 1 (Winter 1976), p. 37.

24. See Cortright, "The Union Wants to Join You," p. 207.

25. See ibid; "Congressional Hearings," *Naval Affairs* (March 1976), p. 11; and Sparrow, "The Promises Men Live By," p. 2.

26. See *Army Times,* 21 June 1976, p. 23. The fears of some who have commented on the disproportionate increase in minorities in the volunteer force might be exacerbated by the realization that racial minorities tend to support military unions. The proportion of minorities in the army is now 30 percent, more than double the proportion in the population at large, and a large number of these are in combat units. See *Newsweek,* 28 March 1977, p. 21.

27. See the example quoted in "Unions in the Military," *AEI Defense Review,* no. 1 (February 1977), pp. 26-29.

28. *Army Times,* 28 February 1977, p. 3.

29. *Army Times,* 14 March 1977, pp. 8, 12.

30. *Army Times,* 7 March 1977, p. 8.

31. *Army Times,* 1 November 1976, p. 20.

32. St. Louis Post Dispatch, 19-20 March 1977, p. 1.

33. *Army Times,* 21 February 1977, p. 1.

34. *Navy Times,* 9 February 1976, p. 1.

35. *Army Times,* 21 February 1977, p. 1.

36. See Krendel and Samoff, *Unionizing the Armed Forces,* p. 9.

37. *Air Force Times,* 3 September 1975, p. 10.

38. Krendel and Samoff, *Unionizing the Armed Forces,* pp. 10-11.

39. Ibid., p. 21.

40. Each bill is listed here with the name of the sponsor plus the number of cosponsors: H.R. 51 (Mr. Ichord), H.R. 120 (Mr. Montgomery, plus 1), H.R. 624 (Mr. Robinson), H.R. 675 (Mr. Rousselot, plus 3), H.R. 693 (Mr. Spence), H.R. 1105 (Mr. Nichols, plus 1), H.R. 1381 (Mr. Young), H.R. 1478 (Mr. Devine), H.R. 1623 (Mr. Brinkley), H.R. 2477 (Mr. Montgomery, plus 23), H.R. 2478 (Mr. Mont-

gomery, plus 24), H.R. 2479 (Mr. Montgomery, plus 18), H.R. 2926 (Mr. Rogers), H.R. 2983 (Mr. Duncan), H.R. 3069 (Mr. Rousselot, plus 24), H.R. 3262 (Mr. Levitas, plus 24), H.R. 3271 (Mr. Montgomery, plus 5), and H.R. 3524 (Mr. Montgomery, plus 1). All these were referred to the House Committee on Armed Services except H.R. 2926, which was referred also to the Committee on the Judiciary. It should be noted that there is some duplication among cosponsors.

41. The cosponsors were Senators James B. Allen (Democrat, Alabama), Howard H. Baker, Jr. (Republican, Tennessee), Dewey F. Bartlett (Republican, Oklahoma), Henry L. Bellmon (Republican, Oklahoma), Lloyd M. Bentsen (Democrat, Texas), Harry F. Byrd, Jr. (Independent, Virginia), Lawton Chiles (Democrat, Florida), Carl T. Curtis (Republican, Nebraska), John Danforth (Republican, Missouri), Robert Dole (Republican, Kansas), Pete V. Domenici (Republican, New Mexico), James O. Eastland (Democrat, Mississippi), Jake Garn (Republican, Utah), Barry Goldwater (Republican, Arizona), Clifford P. Hansen (Republican, Wyoming), Orrin G. Hatch (Republican, Utah), Jesse Helms (Republican, North Carolina), Ernest F. Hollings (Democrat, South Carolina), Paul Laxalt (Republican, Nevada), Richard G. Lugar (Republican, Indiana), John L. McClellan (Democrat, Arkansas), James A. McClure (Republican, Idaho), Robert Morgan (Democrat, North Carolina), Sam Nunn (Democrat, Georgia), Harrison H. Schmitt (Republican, New Mexico), William L. Scott (Republican, Virginia), Ted Stevens (Republican, Alaska), Richard Stone (Democrat, Florida), Herman E. Talmadge (Democrat, Georgia), John G. Tower (Republican, Texas), Malcolm Wallop (Republican, Wyoming), Milton R. Young (Republican, North Dakota), and Edward Zorinsky (Democrat, Nebraska).

42. See Strom Thurmond, "Military Unions: No" in *AEI Defense Review,* no. 1. (February 1977), p. 16.

43. Ibid.

44. All the following information is extracted from AFGE National Executive Council Military Committee Memorandum " 14/Military," dated March 7, 1977.

45. Some of the following passages are from William J. Taylor, Jr., "Military Unions for the United States: Justice versus Constitutionality," and are reprinted by permission and with revision from John E. Endicott and Roy W. Stafford, eds., *American Defense Policy*, 4th ed. (Baltimore: The Johns Hopkins Press, 1977).

46. See, for example, David Cortright, "Unions and Democracy," in *AEI Defense Review,* no. 1 (February 1977), pp. 30-42.

47. For a brief and accurate explanation, see Adam Roberts, *Nations in Arms: The Theory and Practice of Territorial Defense* (New York: Frederick A. Praeger, 1976), p. 68.

48. See Gwyn Harries-Jenkins, "Trade Unions in Armed Forces" (Paper presented to the 1976 Conference of the British Inter-University Seminar on Armed Forces, Holy-Royd College, University of Manchester, April 16-20, 1976), pp. 1, 4-14.

49. The postal strike of March 1970 resulted in an 8 percent pay raise for postal employees (PL 91-375). It should be recalled that the U.S. Army was called in to operate some post offices during this strike. One wonders what the result might have been had the army personnel been members of a union of federal employees.

50. See Ezra S. Krendel et al., "The Implications of Industrial Democracy for the United States Navy," Technical Report No. NKG-10, prepared under the Navy Manpower R & D Program of the Office of Naval Research, January 1975, pp. 147, 152.

51. *New York Times Magazine,* 24 September 1975, p. 43.

52. See Krendel and Samoff, *Unionizing the Armed Forces,* pp. 16, 154-156.

53. See Annika Brickman, "The Swedish Military Defense," *Armed Forces and Society* 2, no. 4 (Summer 1976), pp. 530-31.

54. The information in this passage is based upon interviews in Sweden with Major Bengt Aspring, chairman of the *Kungl Norra Smalands* Regiment Officers Union and that regiment's distinguished former commanding officer, Colonel Nils-Fredric Haegerstrom.

55. See Report of the National Office, American Federation of Government Employees to the Twenty-fifth Biennial Convention, Las Vegas, Nev., September 20-24, 1976, p. 3.

56. Statement of Clyde M. Webber, national president, American Federation of Government Employees, on S. 1517, May 8, 1975, p. 3.

57. See Report of the National Office, AFGE, p. 5.

58. Based upon a presentation by Bruce N. Gregory, president, AFGE Local 1812, to the Inter-University Seminar on Armed Forces and Society Symposium on "Representation and Responsibility in Military Organization," University of Maryland, January 20, 1977.

59. *Army Times,* 14 March 1977, p. 2.

60. See Gerald Perselay, "The Realities of Military Unions" (Paper presented at the Annual Convention of the International Studies Association, St. Louis, Mo., March 18, 1977), p. 5.

61. There is no generally accepted definition for "good faith" in negotiations or bargaining. See Francis J. Lowi, Jr., "Collective Bargaining under E.O. 11491" (Washington, D.C.: Bureau of National Affairs, February 7, 1977), p. 32.

62. See Bruce N. Gregory, "Union Representation in the Foreign Service" (Paper delivered at the 1977 Annual Convention of the International Studies Association, St. Louis, Mo., March 16-20, 1977), pp. 4-6.

63. See Beal et al., *Practice of Collective Bargaining,* pp. 458-59.

64. Robert Presthus, *Public Administration,* 6th ed. (New York: The Ronald Press Co., 1975), p. 265.

65. Ibid., p. 266.

66. Beal et al., *Practice of Collective Bargaining,* p. 466.

67. David R. Segal, "Worker Democracy in Military Organization" (Paper presented

at the 1976 Regional Meeting of the Inter-University Seminar on Armed Forces and Society, Maxwell Air Force Base, Ala., October 22-23, 1976), p. 15.

68. See Morris Janowitz quoted in *Army Times,* 6 August 1975, p. 34.

69. See Roger J. Arango, "Military Unions: Causes and Consequences" (draft manuscript in the Department of Social Sciences, U.S. Military Academy, West Point, N.Y., dated March 1977), note 18.

70. Ibid, pp. 9-10.

71. *Army Times,* 14 March 1977, p. 2.

72. Lowi, "Collective Bargaining," p. 37.

73. See Samuel E. Finer, *The Man on Horseback* (New York: Frederick A. Praeger, 1962), p. 28.

74. See Moskos, "Social Control of the Military," passim; Segal, "Worker Democracy," passim; Broedling, "Industrial Democracy," passim; Richard F. Rosser, "American Civil-Military Relations in the 1980s," *Naval War College Review* 24, no. 10 (June 1972), pp. 6-23; Adam Yarmolinsky, "The American Role and Responsibility," *Naval War College Review* 27, no. 1 (July-August 1974), pp. 17-24; Morris Janowitz, "U.S. Forces and the Zero Draft," *Adelphi Paper* No. 94 (London: International Institute of Strategic Studies, 1973); and William J. Taylor, Jr., "Military Professionals in Government," *Public Administration Review* (Fall 1977).

75. Perselay, "Realities of Military Unions," p. 7.

76. Finer, *Man on Horseback,* p. 47.

77. Yarmolinsky, "American Role," p. 18.

78. See *Army Times,* 14 March 1977, p. 4.

79. See *U.S. News and World Report,* 28 March 1977, p. 51.

80. See note 45 above.

81. *United States* v. *Robel,* 88 S. Ct. 423 (1967); see the cases it cites at note 7. For other cases and related analysis, see Major James A. Badami, "Servicemen's Unions: Constitutional, Desirable, Practical" (thesis presented to the U.S. Judge Advocate General's School, March 1973).

82. For example, *Atkins* v. *City of Charlotte,* 296 F. Supp. 1068, D.C.N.C. (1969).

83. *United States* v. *Robel.*

84. United States Constitution, Art. I, Sec. 8, clauses 12, 13, 14.

85. *Burns* v. *Wilson,* 346 U.S. 140 (1953).

86. *Parker, Warden* et al., v. *Levy,* 417 U.S. 758 (1974).

87. 4 U.S.C.M.A. 509, 16 C.M.R. 105 (1954).

88. 307 F. Supp. 854, D.S.C. (1969).

89. Idem, at 856.

90. See *Right to Work Digest* 2, no. 1 (January 1977), p. 3.

91. See R.S. Lockwood, "Collective Bargaining Potential of the Military Union" (Draft monograph no. 1 of a 3-part series, at the Department of Social Sciences, U.S. Military Academy, West Point, N.Y., dated February 1977), pp. 5-6.

92. This, of course, raised real problems for those in the military who, early on, were writing on the issues for publication.

93. See "Stresses Affect Military Family," *Army Times,* 20 December 1976, p. 26.

94. See *International Herald Tribune,* 8 January 1977, p. 1.

95. From 1932 to 1935, General Douglas MacArthur fought both Congress and the administration over the military unpreparedness of the United States Army. On the major manpower issue, he won, gaining a fiscal 1935 enlisted strength of 165,00, up from 118,570. See Mark S. Watson, *Chief of Staff: Prewar Plans and Preparations* (Washington, D.C.: Government Printing Office, 1950), Chap. II. See also Russell F. Weigley, *History of the United States Army* (New York: Macmillan, 1967), pp. 416-17.

96. For example, Army General John B. Medaris' unsuccessful fight to save the Jupiter Intermediate Range Ballistic Missile program in 1955. See Maxwell D. Taylor, *The Uncertain Trumpet* (New York: Harper and Brothers, 1959), pp. 140-41, and John B. Medaris, *Countdown for Decision* (New York: G.P. Putnam and Sons, 1960), pp. 244-45.

97. For an explanation of the board's origins and procedures, see Gregory, "Union Representation," pp. 4-6. Note that Senator Bayh, who introduced the legislation establishing the Foreign Service Grievance Board (S. 2023), referred to the high standards of due process in the armed forces as the desired objective for the Foreign Service. For another functional equivalent, see Part II of Lieutenant John E. Kane et al., *U.S. Naval Institute Proceedings* (December 1976), pp. 27-28.

98. See *U.S. News and World Report,* 14 February 1977, pp. 55-56.

99. Moskos and Janowitz, "Volunteer National Service," p. 4.

100. Ibid.

101. Ibid.

102. Quoted in Samuel P. Huntington, *The Common Defense* (New York: Columbia University Press, 1961), p. 59.

103. Ibid.

104. *U.S. News and World Report,* 14 February 1977, p. 57. The results of this survey are not so surprising when placed in historical perspective. Samuel Huntington, for example, found: "In a series of nine surveys on UMT from December 1945 to

January 1956, for instance, only once did the majority in favor of UMT drop below 65 percent and only once did the minority opposed to it rise above 25 percent. (The exception was in March 1952, when the results were: favor, 60 percent; oppose 33 percent)." (See Huntington, *Common Defense,* p. 240).

105. *U.S. News and World Report,* 14 February 1977, p. 57.

106. Huntington, *Common Defense,* pp. 59, 241.

107. At least one prestigious forum has done so. The Fifteenth Senior Conference (June 16-18, 1977) hosted each year by the U.S. Military Academy at West Point, had as its topic, "Compulsory National Service." The agenda included among relevant issues an appraisal of the volunteer force and an examination of the movement to unionize the military.

Chapter Three
FOR A BROTHERHOOD OF MEN-AT-ARMS:
THE CASE FOR MILITARY UNIONIZATION

by W. Gene Phillips

Have you ever paused to wonder that so many eulogists, in lamenting the fallen great, have thought it necessary to describe the deceased as both a soldier and a patriot? Have you pondered the reference to our militia as "citizen soldiers" ? If so, you will not be surprised at the suggestion of a trade union for the members of our regular uniformed services. However, if the assumed tautology in these phrases has caused you no discomfort, you need not feel alone. You are in distinguished company. [1]

While the flowering of our Republic is universally admired, it springs from a dicotyledonous plant. [2] On the one hand, we can ascribe to our society the loftiest and most noble virtues. On the other hand, we can support and defend a ruthlessly competitive socioeconomic system. We treat that substratification of our public policy that we label "military affairs" in a similar fashion. It is the purpose of this essay to reconcile the seemingly contradictory existence of a self-sacrificing ethic in our armed forces dedicated to "duty-honor-country" and ever ready to make the supreme sacrifice in war with the self-styled philosophy of the labor movement which demands a "piece of the pie." [3] It is hoped that this effort will help to make the "collective psyche" to uncomfortable to ignore the patent injustice of one of its most venerable totems [4] ; one does not slay institutional dragons without offending them. At the very least, the *prima facie* case for a military union will make it clear that, thus far, there has been little substance to the argument for prohibiting them.

ANALYZING THE OPPOSITION

First, to enlarge on the preceding statement, no argument in favor of organizing the military can overlook the absolutism cymbal that crashes with certain repetition throughout all of the rhetoric of the opposition. Nowhere in the records of public debate is there such an obdurate, unrelenting, total reliance on the "conventional wisdom." The absurdity of the most enlightened and civil rights-conscious body politic since the Golden Age of the Greeks accepting without question the pronouncements by our political-military-industrial oligarchy that theirs is the only truth defies explanation. The erudite Senator Strom Thurmond, Republican from South

Carolina, has assumed the position of chief antagonist and speaks out stridently in the first *AEI Defense Review* against military unions. [5] He also leads the host of sponsors of Senate Bill 274 which he introduced to the Ninety-fifth Congress in January 1977. [6]

The essence of the case against military unions, however lacking in substance it might be, seems clear enough. It can be briefed as follows:

The United States must maintain a strong national defense for the foreseeable future. Constitutionally as well as traditionally, such a defense should include regular, permanent, full-time professional land, sea and air contingents organized and administered in isolation from the rest of society according to the contemporary concept of military forces. [7]

That concept assigns five basic characteristics to the preferred military establishment, although the relative importance of each attribute varies in accordance with the perceptions and convictions of different individuals within our society. These characteristics are: (1) *commitment to the profession of arms,* which is commonly construed to include a waiver of individual rights; (2) *dedication to the mission of national defense,* which entails limiting the societal role of the armed forces to the single purpose of making war; (3) *political neutrality under the de facto "separate but equal" doctrine of our government,* reflecting the presumed docility of the military profession and the possiblity that soldiers might one day vote the way they are told to vote by their commanders; (4) *reliability,* declared perhaps wistfully in the motto of the Marine Corps: *semper fidelis,* meaning "always faithful"; and (5) *responsiveness,* which in the public eye means that this instrument of national policy must be immediately at hand, its cutting edge always honed to razor sharpness and poised to execute the will of the people.

From this perspective, the current military dogma goes on to invoke both the ancient right of a nation-state to survival and the utilitarian theory that a society has the privilege to subordinate certain rights of its individual members in the collective interest. This rationale is then linked to the character of labor unions, which are seen as antithetical to the popular concept of a military organization. In this context, a military union would result in ". . .loyalty divided between the chain of command and a union." [8] The idea of a military union is also considered seditious in itself because collective action to protect its membership is the fundamental purpose of organizing a union. The collective action envisioned by the opposition is the strike, while the protection offered by union membership would encourage disobedience and subvert discipline, thus impairing the efficiency of the military. This oversimplification presumes that the relative efficiency of the armed forces is the primary determinant of success or failure in international war, and, therefore, any degradation of efficiency in the armed forces constitutes an unacceptable risk to the nation.

Beyond this basic line of syllogistic reasoning, three additional reasons are often put forth to "justify" denying the right of our uniformed men and women to join labor unions. The most frequently quoted reason is that adequate protection of the individual rights of service people is already provided by the military departments themselves. This protection includes appeals through the chain of command from the squad leader to the chief of staff; the availability of grievance procedures through the Inspector General system; military service associations dedicated to protecting their members' well-being; and the private right to communicate with members of Congress or even the White House, which is said to give the individual a public voice.

Second, opponents of military unions almost always appeal to the tired taxpayer by citing the probability of an increase in the cost of the end product to the consumer [9], although this is seldom given as the primary reason for resistance to the labor movement in the public service area. Opposition rhetoric attempts to distract the public from the justifiable economic demands of labor while conjuring up horror situations, as in the manner of a recent mailing by Senator Jessie Helms of North Carolina. The enclosure, with Senator Helms' letter, prefaces this attempt at fund-raising by asking the recipient to imagine his home in flames as the fire department phone keeps ringing and his loved ones burn because the firemen are on strike. [10] No mention was made of the intolerable working conditions and career frustrations which caused the srtike.

The third, and perhaps the most persuasive, argument for permitting the admittedly undemocratic oppression of our sons and daughters in uniform is the fear that their union would demand a voice in foreign affairs. In those instances where that voice differed with the administration then in power, the apparent fissure in our national solidarity would weaken the credibility of the chief executive in dealing with other governments. Besides having an undeniable element of truth in it, this is a particularly effective tack because it can be summed up with a word that has proven propaganda value: "subversion."

REFUTING SOME MYTHS

In its common usage the charge of subversion has become synonymous with treason. It has been a long-time favorite in the vocabulary of administrations seeking to intimidate their opposition. Nothwithstanding the unsavoriness of this connotation, our democracy has never been able to speak with a single voice, and foreign policy often lags behind the public consensus. In addition, unions are *people,* and when unions such as the American Federation of Government Employees speak on public issues, we must assume until proven wrong that their voice is the collective voice of their membership—no more and no less, and certainly not "subversive." In spite of the Vietnam era's very vocal doves in and out of uniform, for example, the erosion of support in the armed forces for the successive Johnson-Nixon administrations' foreign policies can be shown to parallel closely the overall trend in public thinking. [11] Most veterans will remember the congressmen and senators whose efforts to subvert the foreign policies of Presidents Johnson and Nixon most likely gave far greater solace to our enemies than did the pronouncements of labor leaders and the antics of coffee-shop dissidents in uniform.

Our nation's political uniqueness is most remarkable for the very processes by which it resolves its internal conflicts and, in turn, assumes its international posture. Military trade unions will not change the basic nature of these processes. To the contrary, including the military in the polling of public opinion will help to legitimize any claims a political leader might have to a popular mandate. A military union may well be a very positive echo of the administration's policies, thus adding needed credibility to our foreign policy. But even acknowledging that the pressures an organized military community might exert on foreign policy *could* embarrass the president does not invalidate military unionism. Executive action without a clear popular mandate, as well as an ambivalent American image abroad, is neither recent nor rare and can be tolerated. But the possibility that differences might exist between military unions and the administration also emphasizes the need to sort out our priorities: Do we as a nation really subscribe to the three fundamental democratic ideals of individual liberty, limited government, and majority rule? Or, is it really a welfare state for the masses managed by a benevolent elite that we seek? The more democratic way necessarily involves more risks, but that does not mean that the democratic way should be rejected.

ANALYZING THE SUPPORT

The temptation in both camps to editorialize is irresistible, of course; yet, the edge in objectivity appears to belong to the articulate spokesman and national president of the American Federation of Government Employees, Kennth T. Blaylock. With magnificent restraint, he discounted union "bossism" when he said:

A union is created by conditions that bring the individual workers concerned to the level of active association and collective action.
....
It is a self-generating process. No supersalesman or cunning charlatan has ever created a free American trade union. . . . [12]

The turbulent course that the labor movement has traced through the pages of American history, indeed, through the history of man, is well known. Blaylock makes little attempt to refute the demagoguery, but instead addresses himself to practical problems which he sees in organizing the military. After his AFL-CIO affiliated union passed a qualified resolution to accept military personnel into membership, the AFGE president directed his vice presidents to study the issue. Not satisfied with the initial effort, he sent the committee back to take a hard look at the mechanics of operating such an organization. In the interim, while scrutinizing the essential aspects of the proposed operation, he deferred acceptance of membership applications from soldiers, sailors, and airmen. [13]

On March 7, 1977, the AFGE released the candid committee report and recommendation accepted by the union's National Executive Council. Briefly, the committee recommended, and the council adopted, a program with limited objectives in consonance with the restraint advocated by Mr. Blaylock and the traditional low profile maintained by the AFGE since its inception. Concluding that organization of the military was feasible as well as inevitable, the report disposes of the "steward in the foxhole" argument by volunteering to accept suspension of recognition when Congress declares a national emergency. Continuing in a conciliatory vein, the committee stated that union representation "would not involve tactical operations but relate to living and duty assignments not of a direct combat nature." [14] The report concludes with an explanation of the AFGE's intent in the fields of legal representation, lobbying, pay, retirement and union benefits for its military membership if and when the present civilian membership returns a favorable verdict on the proposed methodology. There are some problems to be worked out which stem from present differences in personnel and manpower policies of the government in administering the military vis-a-vis the federal Civil Service. These conflicts are thought to be relatively minor and manageable. In any event, they are not relevant to the basic decision to organize the military, but simply whether or not the AFGE or any existing labor union should or can do so. As such, these matters are outside the scope of this discussion.

A hard-line unionist would find the climate in the AFGE offices quiescent, in the sense that there is none of the militancy one would expect in a crusade of historic significance. A casual visitor might easily mistake this restraint as indicative of a "company union." However, a few minutes spent in conversation with the union leaders and perusal of the news release files will dispel any notion that the AFGE is a captive of management.

The "soft voice and big stick" approach is evidenced by the forthright, it not sympathetic, analysis made by Clyde M. Webber in testimony before the Defense Manpower Commission in August 1975 of the problems that the Nixon-Ford administrations had with the 1970 Federal Comparability Act. The late AFGE national president frankly pointed out the dramatic and direct effect of a federal employee pay increase on the costs of government. He testified that the cost to the government of a one per cent pay increase for Civil Service and military personnel is approximately $450 million. Nevertheless, he pressed home the point of equity and disclosed the strategy used in defeating the administration's "alternate pay plan" in 1974. Webber reported to the commission that he had solicited the support of the military in the fight by circulating several hundred thousand handbills to members of the military. This effort was apparently rewarded by "a heavy letter writing effort on the part of uniformed military people [to members of the Senate]." The Senate resolution was supported by almost two-thirds of its members.

This episode serves to counter several of the charges made by the opponents of military labor unions: First, it flatly contradicts the charge by the Association of the U.S. Army that military unionism is a "hoax and deception." [15] In its position paper the AUSA denied that a military labor union could provide an effective voice for the serviceman in the national forum. The defeat of the president's effort to delay the pay increase in 1974 attests that a coalition of the nearly one-half million civilian members of the AFGE and its predicatable share of the two-plus million men and women in the armed forces can have significant impact on congressional decisions. Second, it is clear that major reform can be achieved by collective action using bold, aggressive techniques without resorting to strikes. These techniques, such as distributing handbills to mobilize opinion, would be completely out of character for the establishment-oriented "professional" associations of the various services. Third, there is nothing in the public record to suggest that this classic example of collective action encouraged anarchy in the armed forces. A pay increase has never been known to hurt morale in the armed forces, nor has the same tactic been used since to make unreasonable demands. Professional associations such as the AUSA may call the concept of a military union a hoax, but the record of successes by American labor organizations speaks for itself.

APPEAL TO REASON

Neither the AUSA nor its sister organizations really represent the enlisted rank and file of the armed services. The fact, for example, that the AUSA leaders in their own words "are the army" (that is, the military establishment!) emphasizes the need for the rank and file to seek an outside voice in support of their interests. Moreover, our nation's top military officers are too conservative to provide the aggressive advocacy needed by military personnel to be heard amid the cacophonous demands of other self-interest groups in a representative democracy. Nor can the official chain of command, up to and including the president in his capacity as commander in chief, claim to speak for the last file in the rear rank. To argue differently is to deny the very principles that have made our form of democracy functional. Where, for instance, is the protection against tyranny? What happens to the limited social contract theory? [16]

Pragmatically, the perceptions of the majority of individual servicemen are more nearly aligned with those of the working class than they are with those of the white-collar employee. While the white-collar worker may have some appreciation for the problems of management because of his proximity to that level, the common laborer is far less likely to be impressed with the rigors of administration, competion in the marketplace, or the need for a fair return on capital investment. In similar fashion, the lower grades of enlisted personnel are not sympathetic to the more subtle logistical considerations that impinge on the quality of their field rations. In both of these situations, the basic function of first-line supervisors is to "get the job done." This consideration is reflected in the military organizations' traditional dedication to accomplishment of the mission. Even in the shorter range, an operational objective is given priority over the physiological and psychological comfort of the individual soldier.

The obvious requirement for the subordination of the individual's welfare to a combat mission is the basis for the myopic insistence on unquestioning obedience. In turn, the prospect of a military union is rejected because it suggests insubordination. Military discipline shorn of the pontifications of so-called military experts (a designation usually accorded in proportion to rank and not necessarily to first-line supervisory experience) means simply plain and simple coercion or the threat of punishment and the promise of rewards. A military unit operational in a war situation, of course, cannot offer the same types of punishments and rewards that an industrial worker recieves. Conceding this fact, however, does not change the roles of the players, but merely the rules of the game.

What must be understood is that a worker or a soldier has certain selfish interests that need to be satisfied, independent of the task to be performed. Management must respond or face the inevitable consequences of continued frustration—consequences which are unlikely to be managerially desirable. [17] Trade unions themselves result from situations where management has not responded adequately, at least so far as the workers are concerned. They are a democratic ideal offering an alternative to apathy or rebellion. As such, unions deserve the same consideration by management as any other phenomena in the labor relations field, and need not be excluded arbitrarily from application to the armed forces. Military leadership could adapt to the new rules without giving up the basic game just as police and fire departments are doing. It is simply unwilling to make the effort that would be required.

UNIONS AS THE ANSWER

There seems to be no quarrel with the proposition that a labor union like the American Federation of Government Employees serves a useful purpose in our Republic. Without comparing the effectiveness of unions to other interest groups in bettering the quality of life for its membership, they are accepted as an important element in the needed pluralistic input to public policy. In fact, the trade union is the enemy of oppression. This in itself invalidates the charge that trade union activity in the armed forces has to be a step toward totalitarianism. Laws have been written to prevent the misuse of power by trade unions, and these can be applied to military unions as well.

Unions are crucial to our system because they are visible and accessible to their clients. Their image is the image of the working man, thus adding to their credibility as the voice of the masses. Their role will remain unchanged in their application to the military community. In addition, the track record of the AFGE, as well as the public and private statements of its leaders, leaves no doubt that it intends to limit its concerns to the social and economic inequities of the military services without concerning itself with foreign policy or national politics per se. [18]

HOW A MILITARY UNION WILL WORK

Military management should be dedicated to the same management objectives sought by all free people. Those objectives are justice tempered with compassion and respect for human dignity. A military union would merely reinforce those precepts. Yet both sides of this controversy agree that the overriding consideration must be to provide the best possible defense forces for our country. With that objective paramount in our minds, and with the assumption that no one will argue seriously that we now have the best possible national security forces, it is only prudent that we entertain suggestions for improvement. Thus, the question of military unions essentially becomes: will a labor union improve our armed forces?

The answer to this question, I believe, is yes. The primary value of a union to the manager in the armed forces would be the self-discipline that the union can impose upon its members. The shirker, malcontent, chronic troublemaker, "yardbird", and "goldbrick" will not find a refuge in the military union any more than do their civilian counterparts in the industrial trade unions. While membership should be open to all, union resources are limited. Those resources will be applied judiciously, as they have been for the most part to date. A military union also would recognize that soldiers, sailors, and airmen are parties to a stringent employment contract in that they have sworn to make the ultimate sacrifice if required. Their commanders have the right and even the duty to demand that they live up to this obligation. A union will not challenge this authority but rather assure that the authority is exercised properly. Any challenge to military law or the authority of military management would have to be made through the proper legal channels. And since those in the ranks would be union members, they will support the commanders by moving through established union channels to correct inequities in working conditions. At the very least, the Congress can be expected to respond rapidly to regulate any tendency on the part of a labor union to act improperly or against the national interest.

Communications between management and the work force are the heart of labor relations. They are also the heart of military leadership. Thus, a labor union steward in a military unit as a member of the brotherhood of men-at-arms will be another legitimate means of communicating with the troops. In this regard, it will strengthen rather than usurp the chain of command. Opponents to military unions, of course, repeatedly raise the specter of a mass walkout at H-hour on D-day or, less dramatically, a debate with the shop steward in the foxhole. This argument shows little appreciation for either our enlightened society or the group socialization processes operative within a military unit or, for that matter, within a legally consitituted, legitimate labor union. It is far more likely that the greater convergence of interests that would exist in a military union will strengthen the dedication of all members of the armed forces to the common objective of preserving this land of liberty.

There are many reasons that can be cited for a military union besides those we have discussed but the ultimate reason is, of course, because free men desire one and there is no moral justification for our greater society to deny this right to members of the military. An executive order prohibiting unionization would be another instance of management by edict and would in itself be an admission that the power structure has no confidence in a free and open society. Yet our nation's history proves that we need have no fear of differences of opinion. Our system actually promotes the public equilibrium by giving full sway to the public's excesses. The military services reflect the mores and values of our contemporary society. We cannot isolate or otherwise insulate them from the social pressures of our time. As Mr. Blaylock said, "Unionization is a self-generating process. . . . if our fighting men and women feel the need to join together in unions of their own interest, no bill or law or force can stop them." [19] If they feel this need, it is because the present system regardless of protests by those in positions of authority has not satisfied them. If, indeed, the armed forces offer equal opportunities for all and equal protection of individual human rights, then there can be nothing to fear from the accountability that a national union can promulgate.

Moreover, since civilian employees of the federal government are permitted to join unions and enjoy the benefits of a great and highly successful experiment in democracy, it makes no sense to deny those same benefits to another simply because he is sworn to defend us with his very life. In the final analysis, a restriction on military unionization would have to be viewed as an infringement on the rights of all labor. It has been said that "the freedom of slaves is measured by the length of their chains." If labor fails to press this issue and fight discriminatory legislation, it may come back to haunt them.

Of course, the question of a military union is complex if for no other reason than the emotions and controversy which surround it. It appears, however, that most of our citizens subscribe to the right of free men to organize in order that they may take collective action when necessary. Believing this, we cannot then in good conscience deny that right to the military unless we as a part of the larger body politic can anticipate without a reasonable doubt that such a union would be a real threat to national security. Thus far, the emotional and sometimes irrational opponents of the military labor movement have not defined such a clear and present danger to national security that it would justify disfranchising more than two million American citizens. On the contrary: if the military union that emerges conducts itself as the AFGE has done in the past, keeping within the regulations laid down by Congress and with due regard for the national interest, such a union would be a help and not a hindrance to national defense. There can be no doubt that the courts would sustain the constitutionality of such a union.

CONCLUSION

This line of argument has led full circle back to the possible existence of a distinction between the soldier and the patriot. One can be either or both, just as one can be a manufacturer and a patriot. Accordingly, one can be a citizen without being a soldier but, in distinguishing between those who serve in our militia and the regular armed forces, we are being asked to accept the proposition that a professional full-time soldier cannot be a full-fledged citizen of these United States. Paradoxically, we are then told that this self-same "professional" serves in the military out of some quixotic sense of duty to the civilian population of this country—including the same people who excused their sons for fleeing to Canada to avoid rendering like service. The semantic confusion is then extended by qualifying the noun "soldier" when speaking of our reserve and National Guard personnel with the adjective "citizen." Such a distinction apparently allows us to bestow on such a person full citizenship. This is true even when the militiaman is wearing the uniform full-time as an "employee" of the state, doing strictly military duties, because he is permitted to belong to a trade union.

An investigation of the facts supporting the need for a labor union would have to start with the group to be organized. The alienation and frustrations felt by the rank and file are so deeply rooted in our archaic concept of military organization that they have grown to be accepted as a cultural characteristic. There is no reason to recite the many problems confronting the soldier here. On the strictly pragmatic level, the list of concerns that the AFGE alone would address is proof that they have the insight to represent the military. To be sure, since most Americans' association with the military is either limited to a predictable short term or nonexistent, the discomforts have been endured by the majority as a passing unpleasantness in the natural order of things. [20] Caught in a helpless web of frustration, the individual serviceman can cry or laugh to hide the tears. These reactions are readily apparent in our national literature, and eloquently constitute the *prima facie* case for military trade unions.

Finally, we are reminded that Thomas Jefferson wrote a letter in 1813 in which he stated, "Every citizen should be a soldier. This was the case with the Greeks and Romans, and must be that of every free state." [21] To that we would stipulate that, at the very least, *every soldier should also be a citizen.* This too was the case with the Greeks:

> O unwise and foolish people,
>   Yet to mend your ways begin;
>
> Use again the good and useful:
>   so hereafter, if ye win

65

'Twill be due to this your wisdom:
  if ye fall, at least 'twill be

Not a fall that brings dishonor,
  falling from a worthy tree.

Aristophanes, The Frogs (405 B.C.)

NOTES

1. President Carter, ex-Secretary of Defense Donald Rumsfeld, Secretary of Defense Harold Brown, the secretaries of the services, the individual members of the Joint Chiefs of Staff, at least twenty-five U.S. senators, ad infinitum, have been reported to oppose unionization for the military. Opposition among the elite, that is, the civilian, military leaders and media editorialists, almost invariably condones denying First Amendment rights to members of the regular military services on grounds that it would impair discipline. This unanimity of elite opinion is a major point in the argument of Senator Strom Thurmond in his article, "Military Unions: No," *AEI Defense Review* (American Enterprise Institute for Public Policy Research), no. 1 (February 1977).

2. A plant with two seed leaves. *Webster's New World Dictionary* (New York: World Publishing Co., 1968).

3. Thurmond, "Military Unions," p. 19, quotes *Indianapolis News,* 25 September 1976, which reported that AFGE President Kenneth Blaylock had stated that other unions might attempt to organize the military, and it was important for the AFGE to "be in a position to get a piece of the pie."

4. Walter Odajnyk, "The Political Ideas of C.G. Jung," *American Political Science Review* 67 (March 1973), pp. 142-52: ". . . from the continuing evolution of the collective and the individual psyche, there now emerges the possibility of conscious harmony—in a word, politics. All the necessary conditions for the inception of politics are present: the self-consciousness of the group and its conscious separation from other groups (on the basis of different totems and taboos); the individual's awareness of himself as a member of a specific group; the distinction, even if temporary, between the rulers and the ruled; the recognition of legitimate authority; the conscious use of power; and a system of normative demands."

5. Thurmond, "Military Unions," pp. 15-30.

6. Ibid. The text of S. 274 is presented in the appendix.

7. Samuel P. Huntington, *The Soldier and the State* (New York: Columbia University Press, 1961), p. 143.

8. Thurmond, "Military Unions," p. 25.

9. *U.S. News & World Report,* 28 March 1977, p. 51: quotes Representative Robin Beard (R-Tenn.) as saying that "unionization would almost certainly drive these (personnel) costs even higher."

10. Letter, undated except for "Tuesday," accompanied by enclosed letter from *Americans against Union Control of Government,* "a division of the Public Service Research Council," Vienna, Va.

11. David Cortright, *Soldiers in Revolt* (Garden City, N.Y.: Anchor Press/Doubleday, 1975), pp. 138-86.

12. Quoted in John Cramer, "There's Not Much Chance of Employee Unions Organizing the Military," *The Washington Post,* 27 February 1977.

13. "Statement of Kenneth Blaylock, President, AFGE, on Organizing Military Personnel," *AFGE News Service,* 9 December 1976.

14. The list of proposed union concerns included housing, leave, dress codes, the exercise of political rights, efficiency ratings, and safety.

15. Association of the United States Army, *"AUSA Position Paper: Military Unionism—A Hoax and Deception"* (Washington, D.C., 30 December 1976), included herewith at Appendix C.

16. J.C. Plano and M. Greenberg, *The American Political Dictionary* (New York: Holt, Rinehart, & Winston, 1967), p. 21.

17. Floyd L. Ruch, *Psychology and Life* (Chicago: Scott, Foresman & Co., 1958), p. 174.

18. Among other documents supporting this statement is a memorandum, dated December 6, 1976, to AFGE President Blaylock from the union's director of research, Dr. Stephen A. Kocyak; it recommends a posture essentially the same as currently maintained by AFGE's civilian membership.

19. Quoted in Cramer, "There's Not Much Chance."

20. The Defense Manpower Commission Report of April 1976 blithely labels this the X factor and recommends that "no explicit payment be made as compensation for the X factor," leaving the issue hanging.

21. Lewis C. Henry, *Five Thousand Quotations* (Garden City, N.Y.: Doubleday, 1945), p. 260.

Chapter Four
THE CASE AGAINST MILITARY UNIONISM

by
David Y. Denholm and Theodore C. Humes

Before one makes the case against military unions, it is necessary to establish that the case needs to be made at all. Certainly to many Americans the entire idea of a unionized military is so absurd that it is not worth consideration. In a recent public opinion survey (which will be discussed later), asked if the military were to be unionized would the person being interviewed approve of a union shop contract, a significant number of respondents refused to answer questions regarding military "union shop" contracts because the idea of a unionized military was too ridiculous for consideration. Yet it is worth noting that two decades ago it was also inconceivable that police and fire departments would be unionized, or that there would be strikes in these departments. Now, unionism in these fields is widespread, and strikes are far too common occurrences.

There is no doubt that several unions are actively laying the groundwork for campaigns to unionize the armed forces. The American Federation of Government Employees, AFL-CIO, amended its constitution in September of 1976 to allow military personnel into membership in the union. At the present time, this union is conducting a referendum of its members to authorize an organizing campaign in the military. According to columnist Victor Riesel, the National Maritime Union has established an Armed Forces Organizing Committee. Those familiar with union-organizing campaigns will recognize this as a normal first step in the process. The Association of Civilian Technicians already has organized many civilian employees of the National Guard whose duties include membership in the guard units by which they are employed. In July of 1976, this union chartered the National Association of Guard and Reserves to organize all the members of units of the reserve forces of the Army, Navy, Marine Corps, and Air Force. Finally there is a group calling itself the Enlisted People's Organizing Committee which promotes a strange combination of racism and Marxism in its efforts to stimulate interest in military unionism. In sum, there is at the least sufficient reason to be concerned about the prospects of a unionized military and to set forth the case against it.

Armed forces personnel are public employees. Therefore, in considering the case against military unionism, it is important first to understand the case against public sector unionism. This is not to say that there are not some aspects of military service that make it unique. It is only that any objection to unionism in the public sector as a whole applies to the military as well.

In order to appreciate fully the case against public sector unionism, it is important to understand certain things about the nature of unionism and the nature of government. Unions serve the purpose of representing their members in collective bargaining with the employer of the members. In theory, unions bring the collective weight of the employees to the bargaining table as equals with the monolithic power of management. This is perhaps applicable to the private sector where management typically represents corporate and other forms of capital accumulation. In the public sector, however, management represents the elected representatives of the people. In our normal political process, elections transform popular sovereignty into governmental sovereignty. Sovereignty is the power to rule—the power to compel. No matter how pluralistic a society may be, governmental sovereignty is essential to provide an orderly society in which all segments enjoy the maximum freedom to pursue their goals. A system such as collective bargaining, which presupposes equality in negotiations, will never function where the negotiating parties are a small special interest group and a sovereign. Either the process will be a sham or the sovereign will be destroyed, and along with it the guarantee of an orderly society.

Unions in American society have relied since 1935 on the power of government as support for their organizing efforts. The National Labor Relations Act is a law whose sole purpose is to give governmental sanction to coercion and monopoly by unions. Without such laws, unions would not represent anywhere near the proportion of the work force which they do, and they would be obliged to work in harmony with management rather than as its adversary. Public employment is different from private employment by the very nature of the employer as the representative of the people. It therefore makes no sense at all for government to enact laws that create or artificially strengthen a union which by its nature will be its adversary.

A union in a collective bargaining relationship has but one function—to obtain more from the employer than the employer is willing to give voluntarily. This "more" may be in the form of compensation, but may also take the form of job security, retirement benefits, fringe benefits, and even the airing and adjudication of complaints. In private employment, this system is based on the now defunct belief that unions somehow get the "more" from management's slice of the pie. Experience has shown, however, that, in fact, unions get "more" for their own members at the expense of some other part of the work force, usually the unorganized sector. In the public sector, however, getting more involves quite different questions. Because it is politically unpopular to raise taxes, the "more" is often obtained by spending greater amounts on personnel and less on plant maintenance or supplies. Regardless of the choices involved, the essential point is that unions exist to get "more" for their members. The decisions on how and where to get "more" are essentially political decisions, especially in the public sector.

Why should anyone join and support a union if that union is merely a vehicle for delivering management decisions to workers? The answer is simple: They shouldn't and they don't. People join unions because they expect unions to get something for them in excess of what the union costs them. Unions, as mentioned previously, are certified by an election process. They are, therefore, a political entity. Failure to secure gains beyond management's offer can and should result in decertification of the union.

Union officials are quite cognizant of this. They also know that the only truly meaningful argument that a union has at the bargaining table is the withdrawal *en masse* of the services of its members—a strike. No real collective bargaining takes place in the absence of the threat of a strike. It is part of the system. Public sector unions have come to a realization of the truth of this, even though some still deny it for political purposes.

Strikes in the public sector are intolerable for two reasons. The first and most obvious is that they deny the public essential services—services which have already been paid for by the public. The second reason is less understood and of far greater importance. It is the impact that a public sector strike has on the political process—the process by which governmental decisions are made. In the absence of a strike or a strike threat, there are many conflicting interests contending in the public arena to influence the course of public policy. A strike usually has the effect of unifying public opinion, at least temporarily, in a single direction—to stop the strike and to restore services. (The last year has seen some startling reversals of this sequence of events in San Francisco, Atlanta, and other areas, although it is too soon to tell whether this represents a new trend.) In this political environment, the decisons that are made are based solely on political considerations, ignoring the economic consequences.

It remains the case that unions exist as institutions to make demands for "more," that collective bargaining as a system for presenting these demands is based on an adversary relationship which is dependent on strikes and the threat of strikes, and that strikes in the public sector are intolerable both because they deny essential services and because they tend to shift the political balance of power to the side of a small special interest group—the striking union. For these reasons, unionism and collective bargaining are an inappropriate system of employer-employee relations for any public employment, including military service.

There are, however, several aspects of military service that make unionism even more unworkable and undesirable. Military affairs are directed through a chain of command. This chain extends from the highest officer to the lowest enlisted ranks. In this sense, there is no clearcut division between labor and management. A union of enlisted personnel, for example, could easily find in a combat situation that its senior enlisted member could be in full command of a unit in which the union president or shop steward was a junior to him. Would the men, including the senior noncommissioned officer present, owe their loyalty to the union and respond to the leadership of the shop steward, or to the service and follow the leadership of the senior member present? No definitive answer can be given. Yet the alternative to such a situation would be to have such a proliferation of bargaining units that there would be constant negotiations. The privates would negotiate an agreement with the corporals and the sergeants and the warrant officers, and so on up the ladder, to avoid any conflicts of interest and perpetuate the "class warfare" myth that is at the heart of unionism. This would also be an untenable situation.

Even in the absence of any meaningful collective bargaining, unions might be able to sell themselves as "protectors" by contending that only they can truly represent the interests of their members. This notion is in total conflict with the military traditions that an officer's first duty is to take care of his men. In addition, military union propaganda thus far has attacked military discipline as demeaning rituals. This undoubtedly results from the failure of union advocates to realize that, in the military, discipline is not punishment but a state in which orders are obeyed because of the realization that the well-being of the entire force is at stake. Discipline is not something that can be turned off in peacetime and turned on in war. It is a conditioned state of mind that must be maintained for the proper functioning of a military unit.

This brings us to another important point. There is no such thing as a peacetime armed force and a wartime armed force except in the civilian mind. Military units only exist because of their need during hostilities. It is, therefore, imperative that the conditions of command and discipline necessary in wartime be fully maintained in peacetime. Unions which propose to interfere in command and discipline during peacetime and to cease such activity during wartime are completely ignorant of both the necessities of the military and of human nature. It is equally illogical to contend that, because the guard and reserve forces are more civilian in nature, they can be unionized with no effect on the regular armed forces. Under the present "total force" concept, the guard and reserve forces are an integral part of the defense establishment, and they are the first priority for call-up in case of mobilization. It is incomprehensible that these forces could be integrated into the regular services if their command and discipline were fragmented and weakened by unionism.

The guard and reserve forces are also used frequently to supplement or replace civilian public safety personnel in times of emergency or natural disaster. During the fire department strike in Kansas City, Missouri, in 1975, for example, National Guard units were mobilized because the unionized personnel of area fire departments which had mutual aid agreements with Kansas City refused to cross the picket lines. If the Guard had also been unionized, they would have had to violate a basic tenet of unionism by crossing the picket line or violate the lawful orders of their commanders. Whether or not unionized guardsmen would have heeded the picket line is uncertain. Yet incidents involving unionized air National Guard technicians at Pamona, New Jersey, and elsewhere suggest that labor union officials show no more reluctance to challenge the rules, orders, and commands of an essential unit of our military preparedness program than they have shown in paralyzing cities and towns. Nothing else demonstrates so clearly the fundamental nature of the conflict between military service and military unionism.

UNIONS AND POLITICS: THE SEEDS OF MILITARY DICTATORSHIP

As we have noted above, unions among other things are political institutions. Unions are certified by election, and select their own leaders by the same process. However, beyond this, unions exist as political institutions in American society. Developments in the union movement since the AFL-CIO merger in 1955 have established the combined influence of union political organizations as the single most powerful political force in America—more powerful than either of the major political parties. It is little wonder that unions which represent less than 25 percent of the nation's work force and less than 10 percent of the population have influence far beyond their numbers in the Congress and other governmental bodies. They have devoted a great deal of their resources over an extended period of time to establish this influence.

There is absolutely no reason to believe that a union of the military would not be just as political in orientation as any other union. If one considers the fact that the day-to-day affairs of the military are under civilian political control, it is quite reasonable to expect that such a union would have strong motivation to be even more political than a typical non-public section union. The unionization of the military would, therefore,

73

have as its natural consequence the politicization of the military.

This presents several problems for a democracy. It could be anticipated that military union political power would be used to complement other union movement political and legislative objectives. As a part of this arrangement, the political power of the entire union movement could be mobilized for objectives which were exclusively the interests of the military unions. Such an arrangement could have serious implications for the future of defense planning and national spending priorities.

Normally, of course, when we think in terms of the military as a political institution in society, we think of military governments. The normal pattern in the period immediately following World War II and the Korean War was for military governments to be established by senior military officers who had an aristocratic attitude toward their position in society and their obligations to it. In more recent years, military governments have been established by younger officers who had received their training at military schools in Western countries with liberal political institutions. These officers, as they worked their way up through the ranks, reached a point at which their ambitions were frustrated by the entrenched military aristocracy, which they then overthrew by armed force. It is also worth noting that the military union experience in Europe has been not just a means for the soldier to consolidate strength against the officer class. Indeed, officer unions in Europe are far more numerous than enlisted unions and have longer histories of organization.

The foregoing is important because of the widely held misconception that military unions are only for the rank-and-file soldier and that the threat of a military government was entirely from the officer elite. Such a view ignores some essential elements in our own system of government and our method of selecting commissioned military officers. The commission of every officer in the U.S. armed forces above the rank of lieutenant must be approved by Congress. Unions have made no secret in the past of their approval or disapproval of congressional appointments where the unions felt they had a legitimate interest. This is not to say that military unions would immediately take an interest in the appointment of every junior officer. It is logical, however, to suppose that military unions would be very active in lobbying for or against the appointment of senior officers.

As a result, the selection of military leaders would become in part dependent on whether they were pro-union or anti-union in their attitude. Beyond this, it also would be important for the officer to hold political and ideological views which were compatible with those of the union. Junior officers who were career- and promotion-oriented would soon learn by observation that being sympathetic to unions early in their careers made the path easier at the top of the ladder. The long-term effect of this process could be a military with a more or less uniform political, social, and ideological orientation. If this occurs, any shift in public opinion away from the goals of the military could be met with a military response. At the very least, within the concept of a unionized military are the seeds of a complete reversal of the basic tradition of civilian control of the military.

PUBLIC OPINION

The unionization of the military, if it occurred, would require certain changes in public policy either by legislation or by executive order. In a democracy, public policies that are contrary to overwhelming public opinion are not feasible. So in considering the case against military unionism, it is important to know what public opinion is on this subject.

In the spring of 1976, the Public Service Research Council commissioned Decision Making Information of Santa Ana, California, to conduct a national public opinion survey on public attitudes toward public sector unionism. This survey included 1,529 in-home interviews with a representative sample of the American people. Three of the questions in the survey had a direct bearing on the military unionism question. A fourth question measured the saliency of the question in comparison to two other public sector union issues. Each of the respondents was asked:

1. Do you favor or oppose members of the U.S. armed forces being organized into unions?

2. Do you believe that members of the armed forces should be permitted to go on strike?

Table I shows the results of these questions. It is interesting to note that, while both union and nonunion segments of the public work force oppose military unionism and strikes by wide margins, one of the sharpest contrasts is in their different views on these subjects. This might indicate that unionism has a proselytizing effect on public employees and may be a natural consequence of the frustrations inherent in placing too great an expectation in the fruits of collective bargaining.

A third question contrasted two views of the union shop in the military. The question was stated as:

Mr. Smith says that if the Armed Forces are unionized, then all members of the military should be required to support the union.

Mr. Jones believes that if the Armed Forces are unionized, then each member of the military should choose for himself whether or not to support the union.

Please tell me whether you feel exactly like Mr. Smith, more like Mr. Smith than Mr. Jones, more like Mr. Jones than Mr. Smith, exactly like Mr. Jones.

Table II presents the result of this question. Beyond the fact that an unusually high number refused to answer the question because they were absolutely opposed to military unionism, it is also interesting to note that public opinion against compulsory unionism in the military is less strong than when asked about public employees in general.

Another question in the same survey asked:

Regarding union agreements covering public employees, which one of the arrangements do you favor:

A public employee should not be permitted to join a union.

A public employee should hold his job whether or not he belongs to a union.

A public employee should not have to belong to a union but should pay a fee to the union which represents him.

A public employee should be required to join a union once he or she is hired.

The responses to this query appear in Table III. It should be noted that the combined support of 27 percent for some sort of compulsory unionism arrangement in public employment is substantially less than the 37 percent in favor of Mr. Smith's position regarding the same arrangement in the military.

There is also a strong contrast between public opinion on public sector strikes in general and strikes in the military. Those interviewed were asked: "In general, would you say that public employees have the same right to go on strike as other workers, or that public employees are in a different position from other workers and should not go on strike?" Table IV presents the results of this question. The 51 percent who oppose public sector strikes contrasts greatly with the 82 percent who oppose strikes in the military. For purposes of comparison, it is interesting to note that in the same survey 65 percent opposed strikes by firemen and policemen. These findings are consistent with those obtained in related surveys.

Finally, there was a question in the survey which asked that three items about public sector unionism be rated in order of their concern to the respondent. These issues were: strikes by public employees, unionization of the armed forces, and public employees being forced to join or support unions. The distribution of responses to this question appears on Table V.

Table I *
Members of the Armed Forces, Unions and Strikes

	Military Unionization		Military Strikes	
	Favor (%)	Oppose (%)	Permit (%)	Not Permit (%)
ALL RESPONDENTS	18	82	18	82
Age				
18-24 years old	33	67	33	67
25-34 years old	25	75	19	81
35-44 years old	16	84	19	81
45-54 years old	15	86	17	83
55-64 years old	11	89	13	87
65 years and over	13	87	11	89
Education				
Less than High School	22	78	19	82
High School Graduate	18	82	18	82
Some College/Vocational	14	86	16	84
College Graduate	15	85	18	82
Postgraduate	20	80	15	85
Sex				
Male	16	84	15	85
Female	20	80	21	79
Race				
White	16	84	16	84
Black/Other	33	67	31	69
Labor Union Affiliation				
Yes	24	76	25	75
No	15	85	14	86
Employment/Union Status				
Private Union	21	79	23	77
Private Nonunion	16	84	14	85
Public Union	30	70	28	72
Public Nonunion	13	87	10	90

*Some totals may not sum to 100 percent because of rounding error.

Table II *
Compulsory Military Unionism or Open Military Unionism

| | Smith's Position Compulsory Unionism | | Jones's Position Open Unionism | | |
	Exactly (%)	More (%)	More (%)	Exactly (%)	Neither (%)
ALL RESPONDENTS	22	15	22	33	9
Age					
18-24 years old	18	14	31	33	4
25-34 years old	19	18	24	34	4
35-44 years old	23	17	24	27	10
45-54 years old	23	11	18	36	12
55-64 years old	27	10	18	33	12
65 years and over	20	15	21	31	14
Education					
Less than High School	30	13	17	29	11
High School Graduate	23	15	22	32	8
Some College/Vocational	17	14	26	34	9
College Graduate	13	14	28	36	9
Postgraduate	8	15	26	39	12
Sex					
Male	22	13	21	31	13
Female	21	16	24	34	5
Race					
White	20	13	23	34	10
Black/Other	30	24	18	23	6
Labor Union Affiliation					
Yes	27	16	21	26	11
No	19	14	23	36	8
Employment/Union Status					
Private Union	29	15	20	25	11
Private Nonunion	19	14	23	36	9
Public Union	21	17	24	26	12
Public Nonunion	16	14	23	41	6

*Some totals may not sum to 100 percent because of rounding error.

Table III
Support For Public Sector Union Arrangements

	In Favor (%)
No Public Sector Unions	11
Voluntary Membership in Public Sector Unions*	62
Voluntary Membership in Public Sector Unions *but* Mandatory Fees to Union	8
Compulsory Membership in Public Sector Unions+	19

*"Open shop" public sector unionism.

+"Union shop" public sector unionism.

Table IV *
The Right of Public Employees to Go on Strike

	Public Employees Have Right to Strike (%)	Public Employees Do Not Have Right to Strike (%)
ALL RESPONDENTS	49	51
Age		
18-24 years old	68	32
25-34 years old	54	47
35-44 years old	50	51
45-54 years old	45	55
55-64 years old	46	54
65 years and over	37	63
Education		
Less than High School	56	44
High School Graduate	50	50
Some College/Vocational	42	58
College Graduate	46	54
Postgraduate	49	52
Sex		
Male	46	54
Female	52	48
Race		
White	47	53
Black/Other	65	36
Labor Union Affiliation		
Yes	61	39
No	43	57
Employment/Union Status		
Private Union	58	42
Private Nonunion	43	57
Public Union	68	32
Public Nonunion	41	59

*Some totals may not sum to 100 percent because of rounding error.

Table V *
Concerns Regarding Public Sector Unionism

	One Most Concerned (%)	Two (%)	Three Least Concerned (%)
Strikes by Public Employees	44	31	25
Unionization of the Armed Forces	32	26	43
Public Employees Being Forced to Join or Support Unions	30	40	31

*Some totals may not sum to 100 percent because of rounding error.

While public opinion on public employee strikes is the most evenly divided, it is the item of greatest public concern. At the same time, while public opinion against military unionism is very strong, it is of least concern when all three responses are weighted. This undoubtedly reflects the fact that the public does not take seriously the efforts to unionize the military. Since the spring of 1976, efforts to unionize the armed forces have received far more attention in the press. It is possible that the heightened public awareness that this brings would change the figures. Surely any effort to legislate the unionization of the military would also increase public awareness by attracting attention from lobbying groups. The fact remains, however, that public opinion, while not very concerned about military unionism, is overwhelmingly opposed to it. This will serve as a substantial obstacle to any effort to unionize the military and is a key element in the case against it.

PREVENTING MILITARY UNIONISM

At present, there are several obstacles to military unions gaining recognition. Executive Order 11491 excludes uniformed military personnel from those having the privilege to bargain for contracts and grievances. DOD Directive 1325.6 says, "Commanders are not authorized to recognize or bargain with a so-called servicemen's union." Article 1, Section 8, of the U.S. Constitution gives Congress the power to make rules for the government and the regulation of the land and naval forces and to make all laws which shall be necessary and proper for carrying into execution that power.

While no bills have been introduced in Congress which would sanction military unionism, several bills are pending regarding unionism of other federal employees. By a very minor amendment in the definition of "employees," such legislation could be extended to cover military personnel. The same is true, of course, of the executive order. But given current public opinion, it is unlikely that any chief executive would take this on his shoulders without congressional mandate, although President Carter has announced his opposition to unionism in the military. Legislation also has been introduced in Congress which would strictly prohibit military unionism. One bill (S. 274) introduced by Senator Strom Thurmond has been cosponsored by forty-three of his colleagues. The bills make it unlawful for any individual group, association, organization, or other entity to enroll any member of the armed forces in or to solicit or otherwise encourage any member of the armed forces to join any labor organization. These measures further provide that it shall be unlawful for any member of the armed forces to join or to solicit or otherwise encourage any other member of the armed forces to join any labor organization.

Debate on these proposals centers on their constitutionality. It is argued that, if they are enacted and declared to be unconstitutional by the U.S. Supreme Court, in the face of the Court's decision, it will be far harder to erect barriers to unionism. Even those who are strongly opposed to military unionism have voiced this concern. An essential part of the case against military unionism, therefore, is the argument that its strict prohibition by Congress is constitutional.

In examining the constitutionality of these provisions, it is necessary to consider: (1) the constitutional basis upon which such measures rest; (2) the purpose for which such measures would be enacted; (3) the relationship between such basis and purpose and a potential claim that such a statutory restriction against unionization of the armed forces would deprive members of the constitutional right of freedom of association.

Pursuant to the powers vested in it by Article I, Section 8, of the United States Constitution, the Congress has both in time of war and in time of peace exercised extensive control over both servicemen and the civilian population. For example, Article 1, Section 8, has been found to provide a valid basis for:

1.   drafting men for service in the armed forces—*Arver* v. *United States,* 245 U.S. 366 (1918);

2.   requiring conscientious objectors to perform work of national importance—*Brooks* v. *United States,* 147 F. 2d 134 (2d Cir. 1918);

3.   commandeering vessels—*Lake Monroe,* 250 U.S. 245 (1919);

4.   imposing price controls and banning civilian use of materials needed by the military—*Yakus* v. *United States,* 321 U.S. 414 (1944);

5.   imposing mandatory curfew in certain designated military areas—*Hirabayashi* v. *United States,* 320 U.S. 81 (1943);

6.   excluding citizens from certain defined areas—*Korematsu* v. *United States,* 323 U.S. 214 (1943).

Most importantly, for purposes of this discussion, the constitutional authority has also supported enactment of a military law "separate and apart from the law which governs in a federal judicial establishment" *Parker* v. *Levy,* 417 U.S. 733, 744 (1974). Consequently, the broad constitutional power of Congress to enact laws for the government of the armed forces has often in the past supported sweeping restrictions upon even civilian behavior for the interests of national security and more particularly has supported the imposition of specialized rules and conditions for the military.

The effect of such bills is focused exclusively on members of the armed services and rests upon this fundamental constitutional basis. Of course, even the above-cited actions hardly begin to enumerate the full extent of congressional authority under Article 1, Section 8. Congress has on numerous other occasions acted to regulate the armed forces pursuant to Article 1, Section 8, in the interests of national security. The Supreme Court has been especially cognizant of the right and duty of the Congress to undertake such measures for the general public welfare. Indeed, the Court often expressly recognizes in its decisions the validity of congressional enactments in this area and defers to congressional actions regulating the armed forces in the interest of national security.

Of course, it is not sufficient in considering these bills merely to restate general rules of congressional authority over land and naval forces and the deference accorded such authority. It is equally important to determine the purpose which a particular measure would serve in the regulation of the armed forces. Congress was granted authority to enact regulations under Article 1, Section 8, as a concomitant to one of the fundamental purposes of the Constitution: that is, to provide for the common defense. The common defense of the nation remains as basic to the Constitution today as it was at the time of its adoption. Thus, actions intended to regulate the military in a manner conducive to the maintenance of a disciplined fighting force still must be counted as vital to national defense, and the establishment of such purpose for a measure must go far toward assuring judicial deference to the Congress.

Insofar as it may be demonstrated, therefore, that these bills are aimed at assuring the continued security of the nation, they are squarely within the history of two hundred years of congressional action for the common defense and Supreme Court deference to such action. Although the Thurmond bill does not explicitly contain a purpose clause, it is manifest that the purpose underlying it is to assure that degree of obedience and discipline necessary for a readiness by the armed forces to provide an immediate and effective defense for the United States. In other words, it is designed to assure the ability of the army to carry out effectively its primary purpose of defending the United States in time of armed conflict.

Congress may determine that the armed forces depend for their effectiveness upon an absolute discipline and obedience to an established chain of command, and that bargaining or even the formation of purported bargaining units within the armed forces over conditions such as wages, rates of pay, duty hours, and working conditions would seriously inhibit, if not destroy, the combat readiness of the armed forces. That is, Congress may find and conclude that even the existence of an organization composed of servicemen desirous of bargaining over such terms would be counterproductive to the preparedness of the army for its primary function of fighting in the defense of the United States. Indeed, the purpose of legislation prohibiting the formation of servicemen's groups seeking to bargain over such terms and assuring the chain of command comes well within the scope of governance of the armed forces that the Supreme Court has recognized as necessary for national security. The necessity for certainty of discipline and response to command is not less in the present-day armed forces, and certainly a congressional enactment to assure such discipline would be only recognition of the absolute necessity of such discipline for the sake of the nation's security.

There is, then, a very clear military purpose served by assuring the responsiveness of the armed forces to the appropriate chain of command by forbidding the formation of labor organizations among the members of the armed forces. Yet it could be argued that this legislation would violate the right of freedom of association found to be inherent in the First Amendment. Consequently, it is necessary to determine whether legislation prohibiting military unions would infringe upon the First Amendment rights of military personnel, thereby rendering such measures constitutionally defective.[1]

The Supreme Court has long recognized and often stated that demands of discipline and duty may render certain rights afforded civilians not applicable to servicemen in their capacity as soldiers. Therefore, the constitutional basis and purpose of these bills must result in the conclusion that they are valid and do not violate any protected First Amendment rights of members of the armed forces. On the other hand, it has now become established that servicemen do not, solely by virtue of such status, forego all entitlement to the protections of the Bill of Rights. Since freedom of association has recently been determined to be within the scope of First Amendment rights for civilians, the passage of legislation prohibiting military personnel from joining unions might well result in an argument that the civilian right of freedom of association would be carried over to the military and, therefore, the prohibition against organization of the armed services would be constitutionally defective.

The flaw in such an argument is the premise that a constitutional case relating to civilian rights should be carried over into the armed forces. Federal courts have consistently recognized that special considerations of national security are involved in applying concepts of individual rights to the armed forces because the obedience and immediate responsiveness of the military are fundamental to the general well-being. The special circumstances of the military has historically resulted in the imposition of rules and procedures upon servicemen that are different from the requirements and procedures governing civilians. Such distinctions are not based upon a fanciful or arbitrary judgement but rather are based upon the practical necessity that an effective fighting force can result only from a degree of restraint, discipline, and obedience that are beyond the levels of behavior requested from or required of civilians. Thus, in decisions as recent as *Middendorf* v. *Henry*, 47 L. Ed. 2d 556 (1976), the Supreme Court reaffirmed its recognition of the "overriding" nature of military demands which are necessary in order to assure the constitutional goal of common defense. In distinguishing the rights of soldiers from the rights of citizens generally, the Court recognized that civilian rights need not automatically be accorded servicemen. In short, the Court has recognized that the discipline and obedience of servicemen stands as a bulwark for the individual freedoms enjoyed by the civilian population, and that the destruction of that discipline through broad application of individual freedoms to servicemen could endanger the freedom of the entire citizenry.

It must be clearly understood that the Middendorf decision is not a departure from prior decisions of the Court, but rather a corollary to prior Court decisions involving the question of the applicability of the First Amendment to the armed forces. Based on *Middendorf* and decisions such as *Parker* v. *Levy*, 417 U.S. 733 (1974); *Greer* v. *Spock*, 47 L. Ed. 2d 505 (1967); *Yahr* v. *Resor*, 431 F. 2d (4th Cir. 1970), *cert. denied*, 401 U.S. 982 (1971); and *United States* v. *Voorhees*, 4 U.S.C.M.A. 509 (1954), it may now be understood that the Court has:

1. established that deference must be given a congressional determination under its authority to regulate the land and naval forces;

2. recognized that military necessity may result in decisions affording rights to civilians under the Constitution that are not applicable to soldiers; and

3. acknowledged that it does not possess any special competence to evaluate the effect of a particular procedure and to require its implementations over the balance struck by Congress.

It is therefore apparent that legislation to prohibit military unionism should be seen as a valid, constitutional measure designed to assure the maintenance of disciplined and prepared armed forces for the common defense. The conclusion is inescapable that a challenge to such legislation alleging that the measures would deprive servicemen of a fundamental freedom of association would be unsuccessful on the basis of judicial precedents that: (1) recognize the overriding demand of discipline and obedience in the armed forces, and (2) apply First Amendment principles to the armed forces in a fashion different from the application to the civilian community. The overriding military demands of obedience and discipline provide a clear basis for prohibiting military unionism.

Finally, there could be no substance to any claim that such measures, although aimed at a valid purpose, are defective by virtue of being drawn more broadly than necessary to accomplish the compelling interest to be protected. The bills are drawn precisely to accomplish their purpose: that is, the avoidance of an infrastructure for dissent and disobedience within the armed forces. The evil which these bills seek to avoid is not merely the prospect of bargaining between groups within the military command structure. It is also to preclude the destruction that would likely result from the organization of military unions of that sense of discipline so necessary when men may be called collectively to sacrifice their lives for the national interest. Only in this manner can the fighting effectiveness of the armed forces be preserved.

CONCLUSION

Military unionism is not a subject to be taken lightly. Several serious attempts are being made to establish such unions, even though public opinion is overwhelmingly opposed. Unionism in the military is contrary to the public interest because of the detrimental effects it would have both on the national defense and the political processes and traditions of the United States. The surest way to prevent unionism from becoming a problem is to legislate the strictest possible prohibitions against it. These prohibitions are entirely within the power of Congress and are constitutional. The passage of such prohibitions should lay this issue to rest. The future of this country's security depends upon it.

NOTES

1.   For a full discussion of the First Amendment issue in military unionism, see Chapter Five of this volume.

Chapter Five
PUBLIC SECTOR UNIONIZATION AND THE U.S. MILITARY: A FIRST AMENDMENT ISSUE

by Charles D. Phillips and Judith A. Crosby

INTRODUCTION

The prospects for the unionization of the members of the U.S. armed forces is an increasingly popular and pressing topic in both military and civilian forums. Few would be willing to argue that military unionization is not a possibility in the near future. The final decision, however, concerning whether service personnel *may* unionize rests neither with the military nor with the interested unions, such as the American Federation of Government Employees. Rather, responsibility for deciding if the U.S. military may or may not unionize belongs to the Congress and, ultimately, the Supreme Court.

Article I, Section 8 of the U.S. Constitution states that "Congress shall have the power. . . to make rules for the government and regulation of the land and naval forces." Thus, Congress seems to possess, under its enumerated powers, the constitutional authority to permit, to restrict, or to prohibit the unionization of military personnel. As is often the case when one reads further in the Constitution, however, one comes upon potentially contradictory language. The First Amendment to the Constitution states that: "Congress shall make no law . . . abridging . . . the right of the people peaceably to assemble, and to petition the government for a redress of grievances." From this it would appear that "the people" (some of whom are military personnel) possess the right to "associate" in a labor union and to petition their employer (in this case, the federal government) for a redress of their grievances.

If Congress fails to pass legislation dealing with the issue of military unionization or passes legislation permitting unionization, then no constitutional conflict will develop between Congress's enumerated powers and the First Amendment rights of service personnel. However, if Congress enacts a statute that either restricts or prohibits unionization, then a serious constitutional question will arise: which provision of the constitution is paramount, Congress's powers to regulate the military, or the First Amendment rights of military personnel?

Given the range of arguments both for and against military unionization and the vociferousness of its proponents and opponents, it seems probable that any statutory action that Congress might take to restrict or prohibit unionization will be challenged in the courts. Because of the near certainty of a court test, we feel that the constitutional issues surrounding military unionization must become part of the ongoing dialogue on this subject. For if the courts uphold or override a statute restricting or prohibiting unionization of the military, the decision will be based on the questions of the statute's constitutionality.

Numerous bills have been introduced during the last three congressional sessions dealing with the issue of the unionization of military personnel. Some included only limited restrictions and prohibitions, but the vast majority of the bills involved a blanket prohibition of unionization. Also, if the Supreme Court is willing to uphold a broad prohibition of military unions by congressional statute, it will uphold any statutes merely restricting the behavior of unionized personnel. For these two reasons, the constitutional issues involved in the blanket prohibition will be the focus of this paper.

S. 3079, introduced by Senator Strom Thurmond to the Ninety-fourth Congress, best illustrates the provisions of a bill broadly prohibiting unionization of military personnel. Bills currently before the Ninety-fifth Congress, including the revised version of S. 3079 (S. 274), are less restrictive. S. 3079 would have prohibited organizing of and membership in a union by a member of the armed forces who is "(A) serving on active duty, (B) a member of a Reserve component, or (C) in a retired status." [1] Its restrictions on the behavior of the military and union members make it unlawful

For any individual, group, association, organization or other entity to enroll any member of the armed forces in, or to solicit or otherwise encourage any member of the armed forces to join, any labor organizations. [2]

And,

for any member of the armed forces to join or to solicit or otherwise encourage any other member of the armed forces to join any labor organization. [3]

Any individual, in the military or a labor union, who violates this bill "shall be punished by imprisonment of not more than five years." [4] Any labor organization guilty of violating subsection (B) "shall be punished by a fine of not less than $25,000 or more than $50,000." [5]

Our analysis will focus on determining how the Supreme Court probably would rule if such a bill were passed. This determination must be derived from several factors. First, the political philosophy of the judges on the Burger Court will play an important role in any decision involving the prohibition of unionization: will the judges feel that unionization of the military is "good policy"? Though judges and many others hesitate to think of cases being decided on this basis, it is often an important consideration in their decision-process. Second, the Court's attitude toward the judicial activism-restraint issue will be important. Will the Court be willing to override Congress, or will it depend upon the "presumption of constitutionality" doctrine in making its decision? And third, the state of the law itself—its clarity, ambiguity, and "breadth"—will set the limits within which the judges will make their decision.

In our study, we shall proceed by answering several questions that are relevant to the constitutionality of a bill prohibiting military unionization; and we shall attempt to identify the precedent upon which the Court might rely in making a decision on this issue. The questions are:

1. What are employees' rights in the private sector?
2. What are employees' rights in the public sector?
3. What are the rights of members of public security forces?
4. What has the Supreme Court said about the First Amendment rights of federal employees?
5. What has the Supreme Court said about the First Amendment rights of military personnel?

By answering these questions, we believe it is feasible to project what the Supreme Court's decision would be if a bill broadly prohibiting military unionization is passed by Congress.

WHAT ARE EMPLOYEES' RIGHTS IN THE PRIVATE SECTOR?

For the private sector employee, the right to organize and to be a member of a labor union is protected by the First Amendment. In 1944 the Supreme Court accorded this right in *Thomas* v. *Collins*. [6] The case dealt with a Texas statute requiring the registration of labor organizers prior to their soliciting membership in a labor organization. In overturning the statute, the Court developed the following arguments. The rights of assembly and petition, it concluded, are of no less status than the rights of press or speech. The Court reasoned: .

It is not by accident or coincidence that the rights to freedom in speech and press were coupled in single guaranty with the right of people peaceably to assemble and to petition for redress of grievances. All these, though not identical, are inseparable. [7]

Nor, the Court argued, do these rights exclude economic cases.

The grievances for redress of which the right of petition was insured, and with it the right of assembly, are not solely religious or political ones. [18]

The Court did not deny the states the right to regulate union activity, but ruled that the states' activities are restricted by the First Amendment.

That the State has power to regulate labor unions with a view to protecting the public interest is . . . hardly to be doubted . . . . such regulation, however, whether aimed at fraud or other abuses, must not trespass upon the domains set apart for free speech and free assembly. [9]

A reaffirmation of this protection is found in *NAACP* v. *Alabama ex rel. Patterson* (1958). [10] In this case, the Court again defined the scope of associational rights. The right of association is not bounded by subject matter.

of course, it is immaterial whether the beliefs sought to be advanced by association pertain to political, economic, religious, or cultural matter. [11]

And, in all subject areas, any state action which infringes on the right of association should be questioned.

State action which may have the effect of curtailing the freedom to associate is subject to the closest scrutiny. [12]

While the Supreme Court has recognized that private sector employees possess a constitutional right to join a labor union, the Court has not recognized a constitutional right either to engage in collective bargaining or to take concerted action (strike). The rights to bargain and strike are only *statutory* rights first defined by Congress in the National Labor Relations Act (Wagner Act) of 1935.

Employees shall have the right to self-organization, to form, join, or assist labor organizations, to bargain collectively through representatives of their own choosing and to engage in concerted activities, for the purpose of collective bargaining or other mutual aid or protection. [13]

In fact, the National Labor Relations Act states that an employer cannot "refuse to bargain collectively with the representatives of his employees." [14]

WHAT ARE EMPLOYEES' RIGHTS IN THE PUBLIC SECTOR?

For both state and federal employees, the rights of unionization are more restricted than they are for workers in the private sector. The Lloyd-La Follette Act (1912) first established the statutory right of federal employees to join a labor union. [15] In 1962, President Kennedy issued Executive Order 10988 that reiterated the "right to join or not join employee organizations" for federal employees and expanded the right to include collective bargaining. Neither the Lloyd-La Follette Act, Executive Order 10988, nor subsequent executive orders applying to federal employees [16], however, have expanded the organizational rights of federal employees to include as broad a scope of permissable union activities as those of private employees. For example, E.O. 10988 prohibits union shops and closed shops, and states that "salaries and other employment conditions fixed by Congress . . . are not subject to negotiation." [17] In addition, federal employees and most state employees have never possessed the right to strike. [18] For federal employees the Taft-Hartley Act (Labor Management Relations Act) passed by Congress in 1947 specifically states:

It shall be unlawful for any individual employed by the United States or any agency therefore including wholly owned government corporations to participate in any strike. [19]

Significantly, it has been the circuit courts, rather than the Supreme Court, that have thus far recognized a constitutional right for public sector employees to become members of labor organizations. In *McLaughlin* v. *Tilendis* (1968) [20] the Seventh Circuit Court ruled that a teacher could not be dismissed for union activity. In its opinion the court concluded:

Unless there is some illegal intent, an individual's right to form and join a union is protected by the First Amendment. [21]

It stated that this right extends to public sector employees since "public employment may not be subjected to unreasonable conditions." [22] In 1969, the Eighth Circuit Court rendered a similar decision in another teacher's case, *American Federation of State, County, and Municipal Employees, AFL-CIO* v. *Woodward.* [23]

As is the case with private sector employees, there has been no recognition of a constitutional right to bargain collectively. The Seventh Circuit Court has ruled that a public employer does not have a constitutional duty to bargain. In *Indianapolis Education Association* v. *Lewallen* (1969) [24], the Seventh Circuit Court concluded:

There is no constitutional duty to bargain collectively with an exclusive bargaining agent. Such a duty when imposed is imposed by statute. [25]

No public sector employee possesses a constitutional right to strike. State employees in two states, Hawaii and Pennsylvania, have been granted a limited statutory right to strike, but the employees of the forty-eight other states and federal employees have not. [26] In *Postal Clerks* v. *Blount* (1971) [27] the district court for the District of Columbia explicitly denied that a constitutional right to strike exists for federal employees.

Given the fact that there is no constitutional right to strike, it is not irrational or arbitrary for the Government to condition employment on a promise not to withhold labor collectively, and to prohibit strikes by those in public employment, whether because of the prerogatives of the sovereign, some sense of higher obligation associated with public service, to assure the continuing functioning of the Government without interruption, to protect public health and safety, or other reasons. [28]

The right to bargain is therefore statutory rather than constitutional for both federal and state employees. Federal employees are prohibited from bargaining over any condition of employment "fixed by Congress." State public employees possess the statutory right to strike in two states while federal employees lack both statutory and constitutional rights to strike. Perhaps the most noteworthy difference between the rights of public and private employees is the statutory prohibition of concerted action in the public sector.

WHAT ARE THE RIGHTS OF MEMBERS OF
PUBLIC SECURITY FORCES?

Many argue that the special responsibilities of public security forces should exempt them from the rights given to other public sector employees, but the courts, at present, have not accepted that argument in its entirety. Federal public security forces, such as the Federal Bureau of Investigation, and national security agencies, such as the Central Intelligence Agency and the Atomic Energy Commission, were excluded from the statutory rights to join a union and bargain collectively granted federal employees by Executive Order 11491 (which replaced E.O. 10988 in 1969). But the constitutional right to join a union has been afforded to public safety forces (fire and police) of the states and municipalities. A three-judge panel in 1969 overturned a North Carolina statute that prohibited public employee membership in a national labor organization. In *Atkins* v. *City of Charlotte*, [29] the panel ruled that the state has the right to deal with the dangers occasioned by the unionization of public safety forces.

The thought of fires raging out of control in Charlotte while firemen, out on strike, Neroically [sic] watch the flames is frightening. We do not question the power of the state to deal with such a contingency. [30]

But the state, in protecting its interests, must not restrict unnecessarily the First Amendment rights of members of public safety forces.

We do question the overbreadth of (the statute), which quite unnecessarily, in our opinion, goes far beyond the valid state interest that is suggested to us, and strikes down indiscriminately the right of association in a labor union. [31]

Public security forces at the state level thus possess the constitutional right to join a union based on the First Amendment right of association, but the right to bargain is statutorily defined, if it exists at all. [32] As of 1972, moreover, no state-level public security forces were granted the constitutional or statutory right to strike. [33]

RIGHTS OF UNIONIZATION IN THE PRIVATE AND PUBLIC SECTOR AND MILITARY UNIONIZATION

If the Supreme Court, in ruling on a statute prohibiting unionization of the military, relied upon the constitutionally defined rights of association of private and nonmilitary public sector employees, then the Court probably would rule that military personnel possess the constitutional right to join a union (although not to bargain or strike). Thus, legislation that broadly prohibits unionization of the military would be declared unconstitutional. The rights of the military to bargain and strike could be restricted by Congress (as they are for public security forces and to a more limited extent federal employees), but not the right to organize or join a labor organization.

Despite these considerations, we believe that a bill that broadly prohibits military unionization would be upheld by the present Supreme Court. This judgement is based upon the assumption that the Court would not rely entirely upon precedent concerning the right of association in the private and public sectors. Instead, the Court would look to cases that balance the First Amendment rights of federal employees and the military with the government's interest in controlling the behavior of its employees through Congress's enumerated powers. For nearly one hundred years, the Supreme Court, including the Burger Court, has been disposed to recognize some infringement of the First Amendment rights of federal employees and the military as a reasonable exercise of Congress's powers.

WHAT HAS THE SUPREME COURT SAID ABOUT THE FIRST AMENDMENT RIGHTS OF FEDERAL EMPLOYEES?

Congress's first broad effort to regulate the conduct and behavior of federal employees was the Hatch Act. [34] Section 9 (a), incorporating C.S. Rule I (1907) and extending its applicability, requires the discharge of all federal employees who engage in political activities. The constitutionality of Section 9 (a) was upheld for the *first* time by the Supreme Court in *United Public Workers* v. *Mitchell* (1947). [35] *In Public*

Workers the Court developed two arguments which supported its decision that congressional restriction of the First Amendment rights of federal employees is constitutional. First, the Court asserted that the government is responsible for promoting order within itself, even if by establishing order it infringes the First Amendment rights of its employees.

The essential rights of the First Amendment in some instances are subject to the elemental need for order without which the guarantee of civil rights to others would be a mockery. [36]

Second, the Court indicated that Congress (as an employer) has the right to maintain efficiency and discipline within the public service and to regulate any conduct of its employees which it deems detrimental to that efficiency and discipline. Quoting an earlier case, *Ex parte Curtis* (1886) [37], the Court upheld the conclusion that

The evident purpose of Congress in all this class of enactments has been to promote efficiency and integrity in the discharge of official duties, and to maintain proper discipline within the public service. Clearly such a purpose is within the just scope of legislative power. [38]

In *Public Workers* Justice Reed, writing the opinion of the Court, defined Congress's authority to determine which conduct could be regulated or prohibited.

For regulation of employees, it is not necessary that the act regulated be anything more than an act reasonably deemed by Congress to interfere with the efficiency of the public service. [39]

And again,

Congress and the administrative agencies have authority over the discipline and efficiency of the public service. When actions of civil servants in the judgement of Congress menace the integrity and the competency of the service, legislation to forestall such danger and adequate to maintain its usefulness is required. [40]

In a 6-3 decision in 1973, the Burger Court with Justices Douglas, Brennan, and Marshall dissenting, reaffirmed *Public Workers* in *U.S. Civil Service* v. *National Association of Letter Carriers, AFL-CIO.* [41] Citing *Public Workers* as precedent, the Court in more precise language supported congressional infringement of the First Amendment rights of federal employees. In *Letter Carriers* the controversy was the Hatch Act's prohibition against federal employee participation in "political management or political campaigns." [42] Expanding a principle first outlined in *Pickering* v. *Board of Education* (1968) [43], Justice White in the opinion of the Court concluded:

The government has an interest in regulating conduct and the speech of its employees that differ(s) significantly from those it possesses in connection with regulation of the speech of the citizenry in general. The problem in any case is to arrive at a balance between the interests of the (employee), as a citizen, in commenting upon matters of public concern and the interest of the (government), as an employer, in promoting the efficiency of the public services it performs through its employees. [44]

In cases involving the First Amendment rights of federal employees, the Court has recognized a distinction between the private citizen and the public employee. The Court conceded that Congress cannot easily infringe First Amendment rights for a private citizen. But for a government employee, First Amendment rights may be more substantially regulated because the government (as an employer) has the right to promote the efficiency and discipline of its employees.

Thus, the Supreme Court has established a long tradition of permitting some infringement of First Amendment rights for federal employees—a tradition continued by the present Court. Although the Court has never specifically discussed infringement of the right of association, it has provided the framework for a decision limiting association by permitting congressional limitation of other First Amendment rights.

WHAT HAS THE COURT SAID ABOUT THE FIRST AMENDMENT RIGHTS OF MILITARY PERSONNEL?

The Supreme Court has also permitted infringement of the First Amendment rights of military personnel. The arguments which the Court has used to justify infringement of the rights of military personnel are the same as those in the federal employee cases. Additional parallels between the two categories of cases are: (1) the First Amendment issues decided with respect to the military do not include the right of association; (2) these infringements have a long history; and (3) they have been upheld by the Burger Court.

One of the most important cases discussing the infringement of the First Amendment rights of military personnel is also one of the most recent Supreme Court cases dealing with the military. In this case, Justice Rehnquist, who wrote the opinion of the Court, traced both the history of the infringement of First Amendment rights of military personnel and arguments substantiating infringement.

The case, *Parker, Warden et al.* v. *Levy* (1974) [45] involved an army physician who (1) refused to establish medical training programs for Special Forces personnel; (2) told black enlisted personnel not to go to Vietnam; and (3) called Special Forces personnel "liars and thieves," "killers of peasants," and "murderers of women and children." He was convicted for violation of Section AA 133 of the Uniform Code of Military Justice which prohibits "conduct unbecoming an officer and a gentleman," and Section AA 134 in which "all disorders and neglect to the prejudice of good order and discipline" are prohibited. Levy appealed his conviction on the grounds that his First Amendment right to free speech had been abridged and that Section 134 of the UCMJ was unconstitutionally overbroad.

The Supreme Court rejected both claims and upheld both Levy's conviction and the constitutionality of Section 134. First, the Court restated its earlier recognition of a special status for the military and its differences from civilian society.

This Court has long recognized that the military is, by necessity, a specialized society separate from civilian society. We have also recognized that the military has, again by necessity, developed laws and traditions of its own during its long history. The differences between the military and civilian community result from the fact that it is the primary business of armies and navies to fight or be ready to fight wars should the occasion arise. [46]

Examples of these earlier cases, which recognized some special status for the military, include: *Martin* v. *Mott* (1827); *In re Grimley* (1890) in which the Court said, "No question can be left open as to the right to command in the officer, or the duty of obedience in the soldier"; *Swaim* v. *U.S.* (1897); *Orloff* v. *Willoughby* (1953) which contained the statement "the military constitutes a specialized community governed by a separate discipline from that of the civilian"; and *U.S. ex rel Toth* v. *Quarles* (1955). [47]

Second, Justice Rehnquist constructed the same arguments about the special relationship between the government and the military as the Court defined in *Letter Carriers* for the government and federal employees.

. . . the different relationship of the Government to members of the military. It is not only that of lawgiver to citizen, but also that of employer to employee. [48]

Third, because of the military's special status, the need for discipline within the civilian community. This need is so strong that it may be allowed to override the requirements of the First Amendment.

While the members of the military are not excluded from the protection granted by the First Amendment, the different character of the military community and of the military missions requires a different application of those protections. The fundamental necessity for obedience, and the consequent necessity for imposition of discipline, may render permissible in the military that which would be constitutionally impermissible outside. [49]

This is not at all a new doctrine. In prior cases the Court similarly defined the necessity of discipline in the military and concluded that at times it justifies the infringement of the rights of military personnel. One of the cases that Justice Rehnquist cited approvingly is *Burns* v. *Wilson* (1953). [50]

The rights of men in the armed forces must perforce be conditioned to meet certain overriding demands of discipline and duty. [51]

More recently, in 1970, the Court denied certiorari [52] to two cases on appeal from the circuit courts. [53] In both cases, the constitutional issue was the infringement of the First Amendment rights of military personnel. In both, the circuit courts concluded that First Amendment rights may be abridged because of the need to protect discipline and order within the armed forces. To quote from one of these circuit court decisions,

As a basic proposition, servicemen are entitled to the protections of the Bill of Rights, except where military exigencies, such as security and discipline, by necessary implication restrict their applicability. [54]

Two more recently decided cases which do not deal with First Admendment issues but which reiterate this "special status" of the military and the special requirements for discipline are *Department of the Air Force* v. *Rose* (1967) [55] and *Middendorf* v. *Henry* (1976). [56] In *Middendorf* v. *Henry* the Court ruled that military personnel do not possess the right to counsel of the Sixth Amendment in summary court martial proceedings. In *Rose,* the Court spoke of the nature of military discipline:

Within this [military] discipline, the accuracy and effect of a superior's command depend critically upon the specific and customary reliability of subordinates, just as the instinctive obedience of subordinates depends upon the unquestioned specific and customary reliability of the superior. The importance of these considerations to the maintenance of a force able and ready to fight effectively renders them undeniably significant to the public role of the military. [57]

Fourth, Rehnquist concluded in *Levy:*

For the reasons which differentiate military society from civilian society, we think Congress is permitted to legislate both with greater breadth and with greater flexibility when prescribing the rules by which the former shall be governed than it is when prescribing rules for the latter. [58]

Shortly after the *Levy* decision, the Court in 1974 reaffirmed it in another case involving the same issues, *Secretary of the Navy* v. *Avreck.* [59] In this per curiam decision, only Justices Douglas, Brennan, and Marshall dissented. [60] As with federal employees, therefore, the Court recognized that statutes which may infringe the First Amendment rights of the military are permissible because of the military's special status and need for discipline, even though in their overbreadth they would be impermissible for civilian society. In both categories—federal employee and military—the Court has employed the same basic arguments to substantiate its decisions. The special relationship between the government (Congress) and both federal employees and the military is that of employer-employee in addition to the lawgiver-citizen relationship. This special relationship grants Congress the authority to regulate the behavior of those in public service to a much larger extent than it may regulate the behavior of private citizens.

NET ASSESSMENT

Predictions concerning future decisions of the Supreme Court are at best fraught with considerable risk. But based on the constitutional issues that the Court has discussed in private and public sector unionization cases and in federal employee and military First Amendment cases, some conclusions can be drawn about probable Court reactions to challenges to congressional legislation that restricts or prohibits unionization of the military.

Theoretically, four types of congressional action on the issue of military unionization are possible. First, Congress could prohibit unionization of the military, denying the right to join in addition to the rights to bargain and strike. Second, Congress could prohibit bargaining and striking, but authorize joining a union. Third, Congress could prohibit striking, while authorizing joining and collective bargaining. (Such a statute would give the military the same rights as other public sector employees.) And fourth, Congress could place no restrictions on the rights of military personnel to unionize.

In our assessment, we will focus on the first category of congressional action: the blanket prohibition of unionization. We do so for two reasons. First, this category raises the most basic constitutional questions; and second, almost all of the bills introduced thus far in Congress fit into this category.

CONGRESSIONAL PROHIBITION OF MILITARY UNIONIZATION: CONSTITUTIONAL OR UNCONSTITUTIONAL?

The constitutionality of a congressional statute prohibiting military unionization revolves around three basic constitutional questions. (1) Does Congress possess the authority to prohibit unionization? (2) Would the prohibition of military unionization be an unconstitutional infringement of the First Amendment right of association of military personnel? (3) Would a statute that broadly prohibits unionization be so overbroad that it unnecessarily infringes on the First Amendment rights of the military, and therefore would it be unconstitutional?

While the courts have given the right to unionize status for the private sector and for state public sector employees, no such constitutional right has been explicitly recognized for federal employees or the military. If a bill prohibiting unionization of the military is passed by Congress and challenged in the courts, the courts will be compelled to determine if military personnel possess a First Amendment right to unionize.

Historically, the Supreme Court has shown itself willing to deny military personnel First Amendment freedoms equal to those of private citizens. These decisions parallel in their reasoning and conclusions those involving other federal employees. In balancing First Amendment rights with Congress's authority to regulate the behavior of military personnel and federal employees in order to ensure discipline, order, efficiency, and obedience, the Supreme Court consistently has permitted infringement of First Amendment rights. [61]

In both federal employee and military cases, the Burger Court has continued the traditional position of the Court on this constitutional issue. And in Burger Court decisions on the issue of infringement of First Amendment rights in these cases, the Court clearly "breaks" fairly consistently. In the past, Justices Rehnquist, Burger, White, Powell, and Blackmun voted with the majority in permitting infringement. Justices Marshall, Brennan, and Douglas (who is no longer on the Court) dissented. Justice Stewart has voted with both the majority and dissenting opinions in different cases. Justice Stevens, only recently appointed to the Court, did not participate in any of these decisions.

It seems highly unlikely that the Supreme Court, as it is presently constituted, would overturn its own long line of cases permitting infringement of First Amendment rights for federal employees and the military by declaring that congressional prohibition of military unionization is unconstitutional. To do so would force the Court to acknowledge the supremacy of the First Amendment associational right to join a union over Congress's enumerated constitutional powers over the military, when the Court has not acknowledged that unionization is a constitutionally protected right of *any* public employee.

Finally, the only realistic basis for the Court to overturn any congressional statute prohibiting unionization of military personnel is a decision that the statute is unconstitutionally overbroad because it unnecessarily infringes on the First Amendment rights of military personnel. However, again it is unlikely that the Court would strike down such a statute by declaring it overbroad for two reasons that are very similar to those delineated above.

First, to strike down the statute as overbroad because it unnecessarily infringes on First Amendment rights would require the Court to establish the right to join a union as a First Amendment associational right for military personnel, thus implying this constitutional right for all public sector employees. For as the Court stated in *Shelton* v. *Tucker* [62], a statute may be declared unconstitutionally overbroad *only* when it "broadly stifle(s) *fundamental personal liberties* when the end can be more narrowly achieved." [63]

Second, as the Court has permitted infringement of First Amendment rights of federal employees and the military because of their special status, special requirements for behavior, and special relationship with Congress, so for these groups the Burger Court has permitted overbroad statutes to stand that it would have declared unconstitutional if they applied to the private sector. In the *Levy* decision, the Court explicitly stated that overbreadth is permissible in congressional regulation of the military. To repeat an important quotation,

For the reasons which differentiate military society from civilian society, *we think that Congress is permitted to legislate both with greater breadth and with greater flexibility* when prescribing the rules by which the former shall be governed than it is when prescribing rules for the latter. [64]

Given the Burger Court's grant of constitutional authority to Congress for regulating military personnel, it appears unrealistic to assume that the Court would nullify a congressional statute prohibiting unionization of military personnel on the grounds that such a statute is unconstitutionally overbroad.

CONCLUSION

In sum, we believe that the Court would reach the following conclusions about a Congressional statute prohibiting unionization of military personnel.

1. Congress possesses the constitutional power and authority to prohibit unionization of the military;

2. The First Amendment associational right of military personnel may be infringed; and

3. Congress may constitutionally prohibit unionization of military personnel through a broad statute, even though that statute would be unconstitutional if applied to the private sector.

We also believe that the Supreme Court would uphold any congressional statute restricting, but not prohibiting, unionization of military personnel. If Congress authorized the military's right to join a union, but prohibited bargaining and striking, the constitutional questions raised would not be so vital as those involving the First Amendment right of association. Since the rights to bargain and strike are presently statutory, not constitutional, for both the private and public sectors, their prohibition and regulation are fully within congressional jurisdiction. The Court could take the position that any statute restricting the right to join, bargain, or strike is overbroad in some respect (this position would, of course, depend on the construction of the particular statute in question). But if the Court, as we have indicated, is predisposed to accept an overbroad statute prohibiting unionization of military personnel, then it would undoubtedly accept an overbroad statute restricting it.

Therefore, we contend that the Supreme Court *as it is presently constituted* will uphold any congressional statute that permits, restricts, or prohibits unionization of military personnel. The Burger Court's attitude toward the necessity for congressional prescription of behavior for military personnel and federal employees, its identification of Congress's rights as an employer, and its antipathy toward judicial activism have set the stage for a decision on military unionization.

We are not asserting, however, that any future Court would uphold any congressional action on the military unionization issue, especially a statute prohibiting unionization. Past Courts have looked unfavorably upon the infringement of First Amendment rights even in the name of national security and national defense. Some future Court might heed the conclusion of former Chief Justice Earl Warren in *U.S.* v. *Robel* (1967) [65] that:

Implicit in the term "national defense" is the notion of defending those values and ideals which set this Nation apart . . . . It would indeed be ironic if, in the name of national defense, we would sanction the subversion of one of those liberties—*the freedom of association*—which makes the defense of the nation worthwhile. [66]

Policy-makers and those supporting and opposing unionization of the military thus should take two factors into account in their dialogue on this issue. First, Congress may constitutionally permit unionization at any time. But second, because Congress's constitutional authority to prohibit unionization of the military depends upon the determination of an ever-changing Supreme Court, the time Congress has to prohibit unionization may be limited.

NOTES

1.   S. 3079: A Bill to Amend Chapter 49 of Title 10, United States Code, to prohibit union organization in the armed forces, and for other purposes. By Sen. Thurmond et al. 94th Congress, 2D Session, March 4, 1976, sec. 975 (a) (1).

2.   Ibid., sec. 975 (b).

3.   Ibid., sec. 975 (c).

4.   Ibid., sec. 975 (e) (1).

5.   Ibid., sec. 975 (e) (2).

6.   323 U.S. 517 (1944).

7.   Ibid., 530.

8.   Ibid., 531.

9.   Ibid., 532.

10.   357 U.S. 449 (1958).

11.   Ibid., 460.

12.   Ibid., 461.

13.   The Wagner Act, July 5, 1935, sec. 7.

14.   Ibid., sec. 5.

15.   Alexander J. Zimmer, "Note: Collective Bargaining in the Federal Service: The Permissible Scope of Negotiation under Executive Order 11,491." *Case Western Reserve Law Review* 25, no. 1 (Fall 1974), p. 193.

16.   Subsequent executive orders dealing with federal employees and unions are: E.O. 11491, (1969), E.O. 11616 (1971), and E.O. 11838 (1975).

17.   E.O. 10988, sec. 1.

18.   Only two states statutorily permit strikes by state employees—Hawaii and Pennsylvania. But this statutory right to strike in both states is subject to two restrictions: (1) The strike may occur only after all impasse resolution procedures are exhausted. (2) The strikes must not endanger public health and safety.

19.   Taft-Hartley Act (1947), Title III, sec. 305.

20.   398 F. 2d 287 (1968).

21.   Ibid., 289.

22. Ibid.

23. 406 F. 2d 137 (1969).

24. Quoted by Lee C. Shaw, "The Development of State and Federal Laws," in Sam Zagoria, ed., *Public Workers and Public Unions* (Englewood Cliffs, N.J.: Prentice-Hall, 1972), p. 22.

25. Ibid.

26. See note 18.

27. 325 F. Supp. 879 (1971).

28. Ibid.

29. 296 F. Supp. 1068 (1969).

30. Ibid., 1076.

31. Ibid. This issue of overbreadth is critical in a large number of Supreme Court decisions that necessitate a balance between public safety (or national security) and First Amendment rights. The Supreme Court in the past has used "overbreadth" as its rationale for striking down both state and congressional statutes as unconstitutional because they infringe First Amendment rights. While the Court has always recognized the interest of the state in protecting itself and the public, it has also concluded on a number of occasions that any restriction of First Amendment rights necessary for protection can neither be indiscriminate nor so constructed to abridge unnecessarily First Amendment rights. Examples of cases in which the Court acknowledged the need to protect security but declared statutes unconstitutional because of their overbreadth include:

     Shelton v. *Tucker* 364 U.S. 479 (1960)—"In a series of decisions this Court has held that, even though the governmental purpose be legitimate and substantial, that purpose cannot be pursued by means that broadly stifle fundamental personal liberties when the end can be more narrowly achieved. The breadth of legislative abridgement must be viewed in the light of less drastic means for achieving the same basic purpose." (488)

     Aptheker v. *Secretary of State* 378 U.S. 500 (1964)—"That Congress under the Constitution has power to safeguard our nation's security is obvious and unarguable . . . . At the same time the Constitution requires that the powers of government 'must be so exercised as not, in attaining a permissible end, unduly to infringe' a constitutionally protected freedom."

     U.S. v. *Robel* 389 U.S. 258 (1967)—"It is precisely because that statute sweeps indiscriminately across all types of association with Communist-action groups, without regard to the quality and degree of membership, that it runs afoul of the First Amendment."

32. As of 1969, only nine states had laws providing for organization rights, collective bargaining, or dispute settlement that applied to firefighters but not to

105

policemen; "Summary of Labor Laws," in Bureau of National Affairs, *State and Local,* GERR Reference File 42 (1972), pp. 51:501-51:521.

Four states had compusory arbitration laws covering firefighters and policemen. Two states had statutes applying only to firefighters; Bureau of National Affairs, *Government Employment Relations Report,* GERR, No. 397 (April 19, 1971), p. B-5.

33. Public security forces are not covered in the Hawaii and Pennsylvania statutes permitting strikes.

34. 1939.

35. 330 U.S. 75 (1947)

36. Ibid., 95.

37. 106 U.S. 371 (1882).

38. 330 U.S. 75 (1947), 96-97.

39. Ibid., 101.

40. Ibid., 103.

41. 413 U.S. 548 (1973).

42. Hatch Act, [5 USCS 7324 (a) (2)].

43. 391 U.S. 563 (1968).

44. 413 U.S. 548 (1973), 564.

45. 417 U.S. 733 (1974).

46. Ibid., 743. This statement was taken verbatim by Justice Rehnquist from *U.S. ex rel. Toth* v. *Quarles* 350 U.S. (1955).

47. *Martin* v. *Mott* 12 Wheat. 19 (1827); *In re Grimley* 137 U.S. 147 (1890); *Swaim* v. *U.S.* 165 U.S. 553 (1897); *Orloff* v. *Willouqhby* 345 U.S. 83, 94 (1953); *U.S. ex rel. Toth* v. *Quarles* 350 U.S. 11, 17 (1955).

48. 417 U.S. 733, 751 (1973).

49. Ibid., 758.

50. 346 U.S. 137, 140 (1953).

51. Ibid.

52. The Court turned down a request by the appellees to consider the case.

53. *Dash* v. *Commanding General, Fort Jackson, S.C.* 429 F. 2d 427 (Fourth Circuit) 1970; *Yahr* v. *Resor* 431 F.2d 690 (Fourth Circuit) 1970.

54. *Yahr* v. *Resor* 431 F. 2d 691 (Fourth Circuit) 1970.

55. 48 L. Ed. 2d 11 (June 4, 1976).

56. 47 L. Ed. 2d 556 (1976).

57. Ibid.

58. 417 U.S. 733, 756 (1973)

59. 418 U.S. 676 (1974)

60. In a per curiam decision the Court decides the case without hearing oral arguments because it believes the points of law in question have already been decided.

61. See discussion on *Parker* v. *Levy* and *U.S. Civil Service Commission* v. *Letter Carriers,* pp. 94-97, above.

62. 364 U.S. 479 (1960)

63. Ibid., 488, emphasis added.

64. 417 U.S. 733, 756 (1973), emphasis added.

65. 389 U.S. 258 (1967), emphasis added.

66. Ibid., 264.

Chapter Six

THE IMPLICATIONS OF EUROPEAN MILITARY UNIONS FOR THE UNITED STATES ARMED FORCES [1]

by Ezra S. Krendel

ORGANIZED LABOR: EUROPEAN AND AMERICAN

To understand European military unions, one must first recognize that they are part of the traditions of the European labor movement which are rooted in political idealism and evangelical Marxism. This movement, arising as it did from a society which inhibited social mobility and protected class distinctions, differs in significant ways from American trade unionism. [2] European labor traditions are, of course, heterogeneous. For example, the dual influence on the British labor movement of both nineteenth century utopian thinking and the "work discipline" espoused by the nonconformist chapels was not only unique to that country, but also thoroughly incomprehensible to continental observers such as V. I. Lenin. In France and Italy the working classes still are alienated from the mainstream of their respective societies in a manner which has not been true in many other European countries since the early twentieth century. This alienation prevented many social gains, and the achievement of universal male suffrage in France in 1848 as a result of efforts by the bourgeoisie did not have the positive political impact that might otherwise have been the case. To be sure, even the Communist-dominated labor unions have been cautious and conservative followers of party policy in both countries. [3] Yet the French and Italian labor movements remain imbued with a revolutionary mystique, if not a revolutionary tradition.

In much of the rest of Western Europe, collective action by organized and politicized labor was needed to achieve goals which had long been part of the fabric of American society. Gaining universal male suffrage and freeing labor from legal indignities were high priority goals of those labor movements which later became integrated into their respective national societies. [4] With the emergence of industrial development in much of Western Europe a variety of so-called conspiracy and combination laws had evolved as a device to thwart workers from taking collective action to attain or to protect rights. In 1900, for example, there still existed in much of Europe a worker's idenditication book or *livret* in which it was recorded whether the worker had discharged his employer's satisfaction!This passbook, which served as a device to restrict a worker's freedom of movement, was regarded by such American labor leaders as Samuel Gompers of the American Federation of Labor (AFL) as nothing less than a vestige of serfdom. [5] Not surprisingly, broadening the franchise was seen as a means to overcome these restrictions on the working classes. The Norwegian labor movement broke with the Liberal party in 1880 because of the latter's hesitancy on the issue of male suffrage and joined the Socialist Labor party with which it has been associated ever since. In Sweden, organized labor used demonstrations and general strikes in 1907 and 1909 to bring about universal male suffrage. Trade unions in Germany and in Austria were involved to lesser extents in expanding the franchise.

A very different situation evolved in the United States. In fact, there is no American "labor movement" in the European sense. The fluidity of the developing American society and the abundance of political rights and economic and political opportunity resulted in labor unions which maintained pragmatic goals and attitudes. American labor was able to focus on bread-and-butter industrial issues rather than ideological concerns during its formative years. In contrast to their European counterparts, American labor unions historically have attempted to achieve union goals through nonideological political action. American labor also concentrated its attention on legitimizing collective bargaining and enhancing its control over wages and working conditions. By doing so, American labor unions have achieved more power at the *job level* than their European counterparts who, imbued with a form of political idealism, have attempted to achieve a measure of *managerial control* often expressed in a drive toward participative management or codetermination. Since the levers by which managerial control is exerted are often hidden and subtle, European labor appears to have been co-opted more frequently than it has been successful in this venture.

EUROPEAN MILITARY UNIONISM

These differences are reflected in the evolution and characteristics of the various military unions in Western Europe. In addition, European military unions can be better understood after considering the historical and traditional relations between the labor movement in a particular country and that country's government, including those states whose governments steadfastly oppose any effort to unionize the armed forces. In France, for example, there is a tradition of union politicization, confrontation between unions and the established government, and a polarization of economic interest. It is therefore consistent with French history and traditions that Premier Jacques Chirac in a speech in the National Assembly in November 1975 bluntly accused the Socialists of undermining national security by encouraging the formation of labor unions in military units.

M. Chirac declared that military officials considered the unions to be a "mortal danger" to both "military institutions and democracy itself." He added: "The Government will not tolerate the creation of such committees in French military units." [6] And while the Socialists and Communists both officially oppose military unions, the Socialist leadership in its turn accused the government of Valery Giscard d'Estaing of failing to fulfill its promises of military reform.

But what of those countries that do have some form of military unionism? [7] Military unions exist in Austria, Denmark, and Norway. They are also recognized in Belgium, but the procedures by which they may negotiate or consult have not as yet been legally established. In the Scandinavian countries, on the other hand, the relationship between military unions and the government, however stormy its beginning, is now close and of long standing. In a real sense the labor movement and the political parties which they have so long dominated *are* the establishment. In Norway and Sweden, therefore, it is not surprising that military unions are a readily accepted extension of public sector unions for state employees. Between the polarized positions of France and the Scandinavian countries, we find the military union-government relationship of the Netherlands and the Federal Republic of Germany. In both cases, the military unions are not part of the formal or informal political establishment, but nonetheless interact with their respective governments in varying degrees on behalf of their members.

One additional factor, however, compounds the question of military unionism and its relationship to national governments. This is the existence of activist groups which have attempted to amplify their power by infiltrating and taking control of the state-mandated apparatus for group representation which exists in the military establishments of many West European nations. The war in Vietnam and the student unrest in the 1960s provided the initial conditions which Trotskyist, Marxist-Leninist, and Maoist groups in many Western countries eagerly attempted to exploit. Their common effort was directed toward undermining the effectiveness of U.S. and NATO military units by creating a revolutionary soldiers' movement. The nature of these efforts can be found in the words of one of their more prolific American protagonists, David Cortright:

As violent and ruthless as it may have been, fragging was an essential tool of *soldier democracy,* the means by which men thrust into Vietnam against their wills were able to resist military authority. [8] [emphasis mine]

In Holland, France, Italy and throughout Europe, the foundation and constant base for mass soldier action has been the struggle for dignity and personal freedom—for longer hair, more pay, better medical care, the right to political expression, etc. This approach is, unfortunately, a source of considerable confusion, particularly here in the U.S. Many activists object that such demands are merely reformist and that programs of this nature would actually improve military efficiency. These criticisms fail to recognize, however, that the soldier movement must be built upon indigenous grievances. It cannot, in fact, be sustained on any other basis. Moreover, such demands have a way of expanding radically during times of political confrontation. [9]

These radical activist groups, of course, have had little direct impact to date either in the United States or in Europe. They have not been able to build effective bridges to the working classes and the labor movements; as a consequence, they have no effective muscle either in or out of the armed forces. Approximately twenty five of these groups, for example, scattered through nine West European countries, held an anti-NATO congress in November 1974; approximately one hundred persons attended. They are clearly not one of NATO's major problems at present. Nevertheless, it would be unwise to dismiss them out of hand. The fact that activist groups do exist in the military union movements of some countries, often with influence disproportionate to their actual numbers, requires them to be taken into account.

Based on the above considerations, we will examine both the activist and the more traditional forms of military unionism in four West European nations where military unions seem firmly rooted: Norway, the Netherlands, the Federal Republic of Germany (FRG), and Sweden. Norway provides an example of radical attempts to infiltrate a military representational system devised by the establishment. In the Netherlands, we find an activist group beginning to acquire the characteristics of a conventional trade union. The FRG presents in juxtaposition an association which engages in consultation, as well as a militant trade union with actual negotiating strength. Finally, Sweden depicts the evolution of military unions in a country that is the archtype of the negotiating society.

Norway

The Norwegian parliament, the *Storting,* starting in 1931, continuing in the late forties and culminating in 1968, passed a series of bills which legitimized an institutional form of representation for soldiers. Draftees were to elect a representative, or tillitsman, as spokesman for their basic unit (which is normally of company size). Thus, a battalion of a thousand men would have five tillitsmen. They, together with five officers of the battalion (the commander, the deputy commander, the chaplain, the doctor, and one additional officer), combine to form a so-called battalion board of trustees, with the commander of the battalion serving as its chairman. Complaints and problems arising through the network of tillitsmen which were not resolved at a local level could be presented to the ombudsman for the armed forces. In 1968, the tillitsman organization was empowered to hold a national convention of tillitsmen representing all battalions. The national stage which the organization thus acquired served to invest what had been a welfare-oriented organization with the potential for political power.

Shortly afterward, both the Red Youth Group of the Workers' Communist party (Marxist-Leninist) as well as the KU, the Communist youth group of the regular Norwegian Communist party, became aware of the political opportunities inherent in the tillitsman system. Previously, the radical left had adamantly opposed NATO and the Norwegian military and had attempted to avoid military service. In a reversal of policy, these groups determined to seek national service so as to infiltrate the tillitsman organization either to radicalize the military or, at a minimum, to achieve a credible sounding platform for agitprop purposes. [10] Infiltrating and dominating the tillitsman organization were relatively easy. A company tillitsman is elected at the end of the first week the draftees spend in camp. Thus, a trained, dedicated radical could easily be elected because it is rare for the average draftee to be concerned about these matters. By more or less standard radical left tactics, the Marxist-Leninist group gained control of the tillitsman organization at local and regional levels. At the national meeting, eight representatives were elected to form an overall council. Six came from the Marxist-Leninist group; one came from a fringe leftist group (the regular Communists had none); and the eighth representative was a centrist. This council provided a respectable-sounding cover for a variety of agitprop actions. This phenomenon disturbed many in the Norwegian trade union movement. As a consequence, two bills were put before the *Storting* in 1974 to address this problem in different ways; one by forbidding political activity by conscripts, and another by encouraging an open competition of political ideas. Yet the future course of the Norwegian military representational system remains uncertain.

The Netherlands

In the Netherlands, there is no system similar to the Norwegian tillitsman organization. The political ferment among Dutch youth which gave rise to the provos in Amsterdam encouraged, by 1960, the emergence of the Organization of Conscripted Soldiers (VVDM) and the Union of Conscripted Soldiers (BVD, which now has perhaps six hundred members). The VVDM is one of the twelve recognized soldiers' organizations which can engage in top level joint consultation with the Defense Ministry. Joint consultation is defined by the Dutch as an institution through which elected representatives of officers, enlisted men, and conscripts consult with representatives of the Defense Ministry on matters of general importance to personnel such as wages, conditions of work, and welfare before competent authorities make a decision. The advice of these committees is not binding, and thus they cannot be said to negotiate in the collective bargaining sense. They do approach what is in effect a weak form of collective bargaining. Table I lists the recognized soldiers' groups that engage in joint consultation. [11]

None of these organizations is, in fact, a trade union, since none is allowed to negotiate pay and working conditions. In addition, since both the VVDM and the BVD are associations of conscripts, it is extremely difficult for them to maintain the degree of institutional continuity and sense of commitment essential to effective union activity. The BVD in particular is more of an activist/leftist group with a highly political stance that sets it apart from the recognized soldiers' organizations. The VVDM, on the other hand, addresses the interests and needs of the conscripts from a variety of political and economic points of view. The most immediate issue confronting the VVDM's leaders is whether they should limit themselves to the promotion of the direct material interests of the conscripts, or occupy themselves explicitly with a clearly defined political position. Long-term interests include issues such as the democratization of the armed forces, greater freedom of expression for conscripts, and improvement of their legal status. [12] As part of its effort to democratize the armed services further, VVDM staunchly supports conscription and opposes an all-volunteer force. It also has separated itself from many of the leftist/activist positions of its earlier years and has begun to focus its concern on conventional trade union issues such as wages and working conditions. [13] The VVDM does not, however, have links to the Dutch labor movement, and the nature of the VVDM is such that it is doubtful that such links will be forged. The notion that the role of a student or a conscript can be considered as an occupation is too remote from role models accepted by members of organized labor to allow for any but transient contacts between it and the VVDM.

Federal Republic of Germany

A basic concern of most trade union movements is the establishment of improved procedures by which workers' grievances may be heard. A desire for achieving this end exists in the armed forces of the Federal Republic of Germany (FRG). Analogous to that of the early Norwegian tillitsman is the institution of the elected representative of the soldiers, known as the *Vertrauensmann*. In effect, this is a formalized grievance procedure. In a weak sense, the soldiers' representatives are a military response to the pressures for codeterminism seen in industry. Only an incompetent would fail to sense or would ignore the attitudes of the men in

Table I

Organization	Year of Founding	Members as of January 1, 1976
Association of Naval Officers	1947	3,300
Association of Officers of the Royal Netherlands Army and the Royal Netherlands Air Force	1910	2,600
General Christian Officers Association (a consolidation of two different groups occurred in 1971)	1900/1919	1,500
General Association of Netherlands Reserve Officers	1917	2,000
Association to Protect and Support the Interests of Naval and Former Naval Personnel not holding an officer's rank	1901	15,700
Association of the Military Police	1907	4,100
"Ons Beland" Royal Association of NCO's	1898	7,800
Christian Association of Military Personnel	1902	5,000
"St. Martinus," Roman Catholic Association of Military Personnel under the rank of second lieutenant	1911	6,300
National Corporals Association	1965	5,600
General Association of Netherlands Soldiers	1972	6,700
Organization of Conscripted Soldiers (VVDM)	1966	27,300

his command. The question is: Should such a procedure be institutionalized in the military and, if so, under what conditions and how?

One possible answer to this question is obviously the unionization of the armed forces. Military unions had their effective beginning in the FRG after a two-year legal dispute which ended on August 1, 1966, with a Defense Ministry decree permitting the unions to recruit on military bases. The impetus behind the German Trade Union Federation's (DGB) interest in achieving a trade union presence in the armed forces of the FRG arose principally from the DGB's commitment to strengthening democracy in the institutions of the FRG, and particularly in the military. Far less importance was attached by the DGB to the traditional trade union issues which predominate in the Scandinavian negotiations and appear to underly the sporadic beginnings of a drive toward military unions in France. [14] The DGB membership, which is on the order of seven million, represents a powerful force in bargaining that precludes the need for the strike as a weapon by the DGB-affiliated military unions. The latter, in fact, are "cost-free" beneficiaries of the DGB's aggressive posture in union negotiations with the state.

Two major organizations, both of which are affiliated with the DGB, compete for the loyalties of German military personnel and the right to represent them. These are the Association of the German Army *(Deutsches Bundeswehr Verband,* or DBwV) and the Public Service Transport and Communications Workers Union (OTV). These protagonists, with different political and social philosophies, constitute the main lobby for soldiers' rights, welfare, and pay. Both steadfastly affirm their allegiance to the FRG's constitution and the concept of a democratization of the West German military. The rivalries between these two groups, though papered over in public, run deep and lie in the historic and cultural events which led up to the founding of the *Bundeswehr.*

The larger by far of the two organizations is the Association of the German Army. [15] The DBwV claims that approximately 70 percent of eligible military personnel are listed in their associations, ranging from privates to the inspector general of the *Bundeswehr.* The DBwV is not a true union, but a vocational organization of career members of the armed forces who have banded together to lobby more effectively for improvements in their compensation and working conditions. Because of shared politics and philosophy, the DBwV is associated warmly in a variety of ways with the German Civil Servants Association, or *Deutscher Beamtenbund* (DBB), which organized *tenured* civil servants. In the FRG, compensation for tenured civil servants and military personnel is established by law, and not by collective bargaining. Neither tenured civil servants nor military personnel

116

have the right to strike. They do not regret this since they represent a tradition of service to a government of which they are the bureaucratic and military mainstay. The FRG follows the concept of linkage in a unitary pay scale for all employees of the state. That is, a pay raise for one class of employees is reflected in the pay scales of all other employees of the FRG. Thus, military personnel, officials of the FRG bureaucracy, and professors all may get salary increases as the result of a successful strike by trash collectors or train men, both of whom are nontenured civil servants.

The organization that is most competitive with the DBwV is the Public Service Transport and Communication Workers Union (OTV) [16] About 50 percent of the nontenured civil servants are organized by the OTV. The OTV has a union membership of approximately one million and is the largest component of the German Trade Union Federation (DGB). The OTV began organizing the military later than the DBwV, has significantly higher dues than its rival, and by 1975 could claim only eight thousand members ranging from privates to a lieutenant general. The great majority of the members of the OTV military union are junior officers (lieutenants and captains). They come from a still weak but growing tradition of officers who depart from the old officer corp's philosophy and attitudes. Their number is small because of the former reluctance of the DGB to become involved with anything relating to the German military.

A new attitude is rising, however, and many in the OTV have assumed an almost missionary attitude toward involvement in the *Bundeswehr.* This OTV attitude, as extracted from several interviews with ranking OTV officials, is that there is a need to institutionalize democratizing influences within the *Bundeswehr* in much the same sense that there was a need to institutionalize democratic influences in German industry. An effective way of doing this is to encourage young men from trade union backgrounds to become officers. Once this has been accomplished, it is necessary that they maintain a formal operating contact with trade union ideals and not be seduced into rejecting their heritage by assimilation into the traditional officers' corps. The DBwV represents, to the OTV, the source of a beguiling siren song of German militarism and privilege; and thus are the philosophical battle lines between the two groups drawn.

Apart from political philosophy, the OTV accepts current trends in trade union thinking, modifies them when appropriate, and attempts to apply them to the military. Codetermination, or *Mitbestimmung,* is a strong and lively issue in German labor-management relations, which the DGB strongly supports for three major reasons:

1. "To restrict existing positions of power and to subject them to effective control,

2. "to humanize 'the whole of our social and economic life,' that is, the workshop as not only a 'place of production' but also 'a place of human association,' and

3. "to put 'formal democracy' into practice 'in a decisively important sphere of life.' " [17]

The OTV leaders find the concepts not only admissible in a military context but appropriate as well. This position follows directly from their commitment to a democratization of the military. In the OTV's view, there exists a variety of living rather than work-associated aspects of the military where the appropriateness of codetermination is deemed clear. The DBwV, on the other hand, is rigidly opposed to any dilution of command prerogative. The central issue, however, is not *whether* a commander consults with his men on certain issues; it is *how* he does it. The way in which this issue is resolved will influence the directions taken by the FRG's military unions in the near future.

Sweden

Group representation and trade union attitudes toward management responsibilities, job security, and employee rights permeate the current Swedish culture. As in Norway and the FRG, Swedish labor unions negotiate with the state under the auspices of umbrella federations. [18] Of the major federations with which Swedish unions may be affiliated, the largest, LO, founded in 1898, has 1.8 million members and consists mainly of blue-collar workers. Of those blue-collar workers who are affiliated with LO, approximately 150,000 are civil servants. The Union of Swedish Government Employees (SF) is the chief organization for these government-employed LO members and negotiates with the State Bargaining Office (SAV). The second major federation of unions is the Central Organization of Salaried Employees (TCO). Within the TCO, there is a section of approximately 180,000 civil servants (TCO-S). There are ten unions within this particular federation. The Swedish Confederation of Professional Associations (SACO) includes employees and owners of business enterprises, such as lawyers, doctors with private practice, and so forth. Certain groups with lower academic degrees (status credentials are important in Sweden) are also connected with SACO—physiotherapists, reserve officers, and so forth. SACO has about 100,000 members of whom 40,000 are government employees. They are as a rule, in the higher salary grades. There is no special organization of civil servants within SACO. The National Federation of Government Officers (SR), which has merged with SACO, represents about thirty unions of state officials in the higher and medium salary grade, of whom there are about 18,000. The principal groups consist of persons who have taken up the "matriculatory careers," that is, careers open to those who have an upper school education—in the post office, customs office, state railways, and so forth.

It is important to recognize that the Swedish Trade Union Confederation (LO) provides the major financial support and membership for the Social Democratic party, which, except for a few months in 1934, controlled the Swedish government either alone or in coalition from 1932 until September 1976. Membership in the LO automatically confers membership and dues-paying responsibility in the Social Democratic party. Other union federations have comparable links to the political process. Consequently, as in Norway, the trade unions are not mere contenders for political power; they are a significant component of the ruling establishment itself.

Swedish military unions had their origin in 1907 when a company grade officers' union was founded. It was followed by the formation of a union for noncommissioned officers and above. The emerging unions had three goals: first, to improve the salary position of the officers for whom they were responsible; second, to improve working conditions; and third, to extend the retirement age. These goals have been achieved, although it was not until 1936 that the right of association and collective bargaining was made explicit by Swedish law.

Military unions represent 99 percent of the personnel in the regular Swedish armed forces. As in Norway and the FRG, conscripts cannot be members of the Swedish military unions. Instead, they are represented by means of a variety of committees. Each regiment has a committee which the commander consults when appropriate. In addition to this, on a national level, conscripts have a parliament—one or two representatives from each regiment who meet once a year.

The largest individual union is the Swedish Association of the Army, Navy, and Air Force Officers (SOF). The Swedish Union of Officers (SOF) is for officers of the rank of major or lieutenant commander and above. About six thousand military academy educated active officers of different salary grades, as well as about three hundred cadets, are members of the SOF. Nonactive members are retired officers numbering perhaps a thousand. The SOF has about one hundred locals. Trade union responsibilities of the SOF, such as negotiations, are carried out by five full-time employed members of the SOF who operate in accordance with instructions from the board of the SOF. This consists of sixteen officers from the different defense forces, from different parts of Sweden, and holding varying ranks.

The Union of Company Officers (KOF) consists of officers from the rank of ensign to lieutenant and is affiliated with the TCO-S. The KOF has 5,000 active members, 2,500 of whom are civilian employees of the military who have the assimilated rank or equivalent standing of company officers. The Union of Noncommissioned Officers (POF) is also affiliated with the TCO-S. This union consists of 9,300 active noncommissioned officers of whom about 3,000 are, in fact, aviation technicians working for the military.

In Sweden, the movement from negotiations over work rules to institutionalized codetermination is further advanced than it is in Norway or the FRG. The erosion of what had been considered management prerogatives gained momentum in a law passed in 1971 in which the forty-hour work week was established for the military, with overtime limited to 150 hours per year. In the event of a war or an emergency, this limit on overtime work in the military is suspended. Civilians working for the military won the right to negotiate overtime conditions in a 1972 decision of the labor courts. They negotiated a forty-hour regular week plus two hundred maximum hours of overtime for non-wartime emergencies. As yet, no controversy has arisen as to what constitutes an emergency. A common example would be searching for a lost aircraft.

The notion of a limited military day and of a limitation on military overtime appears bizarre at first blush. It should be remembered, however, that the Swedish Army is a garrison army devoted to training. The need for overtime often arises because of poor planning on the part of the commanding officer or of the training command. Many senior officers protested this limitation at first, but the situation appears to have worked out well. The additional planning imposed on management was relatively minor. Prior to this regulation, the union influence was such that the union representative on a post, who acts as a form of shop steward, was routinely consulted by the commander on matters affecting the men, such as the need to work overtime.

In March 1974 the TCO-S and the SF issued a document entitled "Union Requirements and Democracy in the Defense Organization." It is of interest to quote the principles upon which the requirements are based.

A series of measures must now be taken for improving democracy within the defense organization. The main objective here shall be to ensure that the individual's influence within the defense organization shall be much the same as on the civil labor market.

In addition to information and mutual consultation rights, employees within the defense organization must be guaranteed the right of codetermination as soon as possible.

This right of codetermination must be built up according to an established pattern and be relevant throughout the hierarchy of the defense sector.

The right of codetermination shall have a trade union foundation and shall be developed through collaboration among the union organizations. [19]

CONCLUSION

In the FRG, elements in the DGB perceived a need to institutionalize the influence of civilian democratic traditions upon the armed forces by means of military unions. In the United States there are no such pressures from pragmatic American trade unions that are well integrated into American society. The left-wing politically activist American Servicemen's Union, founded in 1967, was of little consequence; *may* have achieved six to eight thousand members; and disappeared in the early 1970s. The argument that a union presence would democratize the U.S. armed forces has been raised recently in the press [20], but there is no indication that these intellectual arguments have the support of significant numbers of servicemen or of the American trade union movement itself. It is even difficult to see why a unionized, all-volunteer military would provide a more reliable safeguard for civilian democratic processes than would a nonunionized all-volunteer armed force. [21] A plausible and somewhat frightening argument can be summoned against the unionization of the armed forces in American society in that it creates the potential for creating a "Praetorian Guard" attitude on the part of its members.

The most significant and inescapable distinction between the European military experience with trade unionism and analogies with the armed forces of the United States lies in the differing strategic roles of the respective forces. Hesitation in the command and control capabilities or a lapse in the effectiveness of the combat arms of a European democracy might bring comfort and delight to Soviet planners, but it would likely have little influence on the dynamics of the U.S.-Soviet military confrontation. Evidence of a similar hesitation or lapse on the part of the United States might provide an invitation to Soviet military adventures and perhaps to Armageddon.

Despite the many differences which serve to weaken analogies between the European military unions and possible events in the United States, four useful inferences may be drawn. First, these military unions have evolved from the orderly maturation of public sector collective bargaining. The behavior they represent is not a freak episode in the recent history or culture of their countries. Therefore, the examination of similar social trends in this country can enable an alert and sophisticated observer to understand and prepare for possible alternative responses to developing pressures and expectations.

121

Second, the "new left" activist efforts at organizing soldiers have been weak, short-lived, and ineffective. They have persisted only when they became like trade unions which were part of an institutionalized pattern of industrial and public sector negotiations and bargaining. We have no evidence, however, whether a "new right," were it to emerge, would be similarly transient and ineffective.

Third, despite national cultural differences, it is unlikely that the goals and expectations of the individual unionized European military personnel differ widely from those of their nonunionized American counterparts. In this event, awareness of the subject matter of European military union negotiations or consultations with associations may help American observers either to anticipate issues that may arise in this country or to substantiate the presence of issues which are beginning to emerge only now. An example may be found in the growing pressure throughout the Scandinavian countries and the FRG for military participation at the "job" level in matters where command prerogatives are not threatened. In an associated vein, there also have been evident efforts on the part of the European unions to distinguish operational service conditions. both normal and emergency, from the living conditions in military service.

Fourth, and finally, the European armed forces which are unionized do not appear to be any the less effective for it. Comparability of military pay scales with that of civilian state officials, which follows naturally from the negotiating precedures employed, is well accepted, and performance in military exercises appears to be independent of the existence of military unions.

NOTES

1. Much of what follows in an adaptation of Ezra S. Krendel, "European Military Unions," in E. S. Krendel and B. L. Samoff, eds., *Unionizing the Armed Forces* (Philadelphia: University of Pennsylvania Press, 1977), chap. 8.

2. Useful background information will be found in: Adolph Strumthal, *Comparative Labor Movements, Ideological Roots and Institutional Development* (Belmont, Calif.: Wadsworth Publishing Co., 1972), and Everett M. Kassalow, *Trade Unions and Industrial Relations: An International Comparison* (New York: Random House, 1969).

3. Kassalow, *Trade Unions,* chap. 6. In the strikes which rocked France in the spring of 1968, the Communist-dominated trade union confederation, *Confederation Generale du Travail* (CGT), attempted to dampen the revolutionary ardor of the students and militant leftists by urging restraint and responsible behavior. The CGT so gloried in this role that it referred to itself in a communique as *"La Grande Force Tranquille."* It would appear that they are more apt to await patiently the coming of the new order in response to the inex-

orable forces of history according to the gospel of Karl Marx than they are to assume national and international risks in attempting to accelerate its progress.

4.   Ibid., pp. 7-12.

5.   The reluctance of non-Marxist labor leaders in the West to accept Soviet bloc representatives of so-called labor unions as legitimate in such organizations as the ILO derives in part from the continued maintenance of the apparatus of effective serfdom, for example, the equivalent of the *livret* in the Soviet Union to this day.

6.   "France Fighting Military Unions," *New York Times,* 30 November 1975. For a useful discussion of this subject, see Lucien Mandeville, "Syndicalism and the French Military System" *Armed Forces and Society* 2, no. 4 (Summer 1976).

7.   *Survey of Military Personnel Representation Practice in the Armed Forces of Eurogroup-Nations,* EUROSTRUCTURE–Secretariat, Bonn, 3 May 1976.

8.   David Cortright, *Soldiers in Revolt* (Garden City, N.Y.: Anchor Press, Doubleday, 1975), p. 46.

9.   David Cortright, "International Soldiers' Movement," *RECON* 3, no. 7 (July 1975), p. 16.

10.   *Study Outline for Politics in the Military,* translation of internal document circulated by Red Youth Group of the Workers' Communist party (Marxist-Leninist) of Norway, 1973.

11.   *Survey of Eurogroup,* Annex B-4.

12.   Walter Kok, *Dienstplichtigen en hun Vakbondsproblematiek,* undated descriptive memo on organization of and issues concerning the VVDM and BVD, contained in material supplied in April 1974 by T. L. J. Brouwer, Col. RNLA, Military Attache, Royal Netherlands Embassy, Washington, D.C.

13.   Ger Teitler, "The Successful Case of Military Unionization in the Netherlands," *Armed Forces and Society* 2, no. 4 (Summer 1976).

14.   Bernhard Fleckenstein, "The Military and Labor Union Organization in Germany," *Armed Forces and Society* 2, no. 4 (Summer 1976).

15.   Herman Giesen, *Der Deutsche Bundeswehr-Verband, Amter und Organizationen der Bundesrepublik Deutschland* (Bonn: Boldt Verlag, 1970).

16.   *Informationen Fur Alle Soldaten*, OTV pamphlet, April 1973.

17.   Wilhelm Hakerkampf, *Codetermination in the Basic Programme of the German Trade Unions* (Dusseldorf: DGB, 1964) as quoted in Jack Barbash, *Trade Unions & National Economic Policy* (Baltimore: The Johns Hopkins Press, 1972), p. 91.

18.   Annika Brickman, "Military Trade Unionism in Sweden," *Armed Forces and Society* 2, no. 4 (Summer 1976).

19. *Fackliga Krav Pa Demokratin Inom Forsvaret* (Union Requirements and Democracy in the Defense Organization) (Stockholm: TCO-S and SF, March 1974).

20. David Cortright, "The Union Wants to Join You," *The Nation,* 21 February 1976; and Tod Ensign and Michael Uhl, "Soldiers as Workers," *The Progressive* 40, no. 4 (April 1976).

21. It is entirely possible that some of the arguments for democratizing the armed forces use "democratic" in the sense that it is used in East Germany, the German Democratic Republic, or in the sense that Cortright describes fragging as a "tool of soldier democracy" (see note 8).

124

Chapter Seven
AMERICAN MILITARY UNIONS:
A SOCIOLOGICAL ANALYSIS

By Thomas C. Wyatt

Institutions are products of the past process, are adapted to past circumstances, and are therefore never in full accord with the requirements of the present.

—Thorstein Veblen, 1934

THE MILITARY AS A MAJOR SOCIAL INSTITUTION

The military has long been recognized as both a social institution in itself and as a large, formal, complex component of the larger society. Professor Elting E. Morrison once trenchantly described military organizations as societies built around and upon the prevailing weapons system. [1] Yet the military is not a closed system. It has been developed, and is supported, by the larger society, and as such the military provides a particular service to that society. The nature and structure of the military as a component of the larger society are also subject to the same general social models which influence that larger society. It is true that much of the structure and many of the functions of military associations have been considered to be distinctively different from those of other large and complex formal organizations. But the structure and functions of the military are composed of, and produced by, men and women who initially are drawn from the host society, whatever the degree of professional or occupational socialization they subsequently experience. Thus, whereas the physical and engineering aspects of the military are different, the human and social character may not be similarly set apart from the societal whole. Further, the more industrialized and "civilianized" the military becomes, the less appropriate it is to dwell on its allegedly unique attributes. Rather than assign the military the special status of a social anomaly and create new models with which it can be examined, then, it seems far wiser to concentrate on its commonalities with other social institutions and avoid the waste of rediscovery.

SOCIAL CHANGE AND UNIONIZATION

The existence of observable changes in the behavior of members of an institution or organization does not necessarily indicate a change in that social entity. Changes in individual behavior may be merely an adaptive response to stimuli from certain internal or external environments associated with the institution, or what one scholar calls *readjustive* behavior. [2] If management assumes readjustive behavior to be either an indication of organizational change, or an attempt on the part of the membership to modify the organization, and takes action to resist or disrupt the presumed change process, the gulf between the two major divisions of the organization—management and labor—may be widened artificially. Such action is clearly disruptive, and can lead to unsolicited, unnecessary, and perhaps undesirable changes in the organization itself.

Crisis situations immediately preceding revolutionary change in institutions exist when some old, routinized, long familiar perspective of reality seems no longer to fit, or carry meaning. [3] Without some form of either adaptive behavior or benign cumulative change, an institutional revolution will produce a new paradigm, or world view, out of which will come a new institutional structure. On the other hand, these small, benign cumulative changes which tend to group themselves into identifiable clusters [4], do not necessarily indicate that a major change in the organization is underway or has occurred. But they do reveal areas of potential change, should other facilitating conditions appear. These indicators of potential change would be important to those members of the organization who were committed to, or interested in maintaining, the status quo of that organization.

In addition, each social system exists within a three-part environment: (1) a physical environment (geographic location, climate, etc.); (2) a cultural environment (norms, values, goals of society); and (3) a technological environment (state of knowledge and instrumentation available for task performance). [5] There exists a degree of interdependence among the system and these environments. Thus, changes in any one of the environments will produce changes in the other interconnected environments, as well as in the system itself. Similarly, changes in the activities, sentiments, or interaction of system members will produce changes in the environment. For example, from a worker's informal efforts at solving problems only of concern to himself may come ideas for technological change (altering the technological environment), redesigned work areas (changing the physical environment), and new norms about the relationship between labor and management (changing the cultural environment). Society is clearly a complex system, and consideration of one of its constituent parts—an institution or organization—cannot be undertaken without attending to the other interdependent parts. There is simply no good insulation between elements of the complex social system. A change produced in the labor division of the organization—from within or without—will tend to produce change in other parts of the organization.

Finally, it has been found that a change (which could be termed an "invention") can be successful in modifying an organization when it may be characterized as a dislocating or crisis-like event for which the system has no prepared response. [6] Schon's paradigm for organizational change described a four-step process. First, there must be a conventionalizing, fixating character of traditional behavior within the system. Second, the motivation for change must come from outside the system. Third, there must be the appearance of a crisis-like situation within which the desired change may be identified and implemented. Finally, of crucial importance, there must be a resolute group that occupies a position of power to enforce the use of the tradition-flouting "invention."

The U.S. military institution can be examined in terms of these models. Consider the fit, for example, if there exists in military organizations conventional, fixating traditional behavior that would be of a nature to precipitate such an institutional crisis. The motivation to change coming from outside the system may be seen as the activity of organized labor to recruit service personnel to form a military union. Add to this the conditions of dissatisfaction related to alienation from work or the institution which might be found among the worker membership. In this case, the second element of Homan's paradigm is fused with Schon's third element—the crisis-like situation within which the desired change obtains. Here, the change would be the creation of a military union, and the crisis situation would describe indiscipline and other forms of dissatisfaction with the military demonstrated by service personnel. The fourth element of Schon's model—the resolute group with power to enforce the use of the tradition-flouting invention (union)—would be the worker membership of the military institution if that membership gains power through organization into a military union. Changes in the institution would be predictably far-reaching.

CHANGING NATURE OF THE MILITARY, CHANGE RESISTANCE, AND SOCIAL CONFLICT: SEEDBED FOR UNIONIZATION

Defenders of an institutional status quo, in order to protect their own vested interests, tend to resist vigorously attempts to make significant changes in that institution. This action is taken even when the institution is no longer compatible with relevant environmental developments. Waste and inefficiency are the consequence of the lack of congruence between (for example) a new technology or set of cultural norms and an institution operating under rules and procedures antedating those developments. The more rapid the rate of technological innovation or cultural change, the greater the demand for institutional change. The period of transition between old and (if they succeed in overcoming their predecessors) new institutions is likely to be one marked by considerable social conflict. [7] Both advocates and opponents of the "new order" ally themselves with those in other institutions who share their views. In the end, institutions which accommodate the demands placed upon them by and large survive those which did not.

For its part, the military touches many threads of the social fabric of any society. Conflict and change within the military will therefore impinge on the interests of individuals in many other institutions. In the case of demands for the unionization of the military, military management obviously will seek, and probably find, significant assistance from the larger establishment in its efforts to ward off military unions. Yet this action could serve to alienate military labor even further, prompting it to oppose management with an organized front and to seek allies outside the organization. This would foster the development of unions within the military.

Military unions, of course, are novel at this time. However, two important factors need to be taken into consideration. First, military societies are not greatly different from other types of societies; what is found in one is not wholly alien to the other. Second, precedents for U.S. military unions are to be found in other armies and, closer to home, the public sector of organized firemen, policemen, and other emergency service personnel among city, state, and federal government employees. But the clearest invitation to unionism is the shift of the military institution itself toward an industrial-occupational model in response to changes within its environment. In this approach, the orientation of the working force (and, perhaps, management as well) is more toward self-interest than self-sacrifice or fealty to the employing organization. Since trade unions and the work community are the common forums for the expression of needs and the resolution of grievances [8], it is not surprising that an occupation-oriented military institution would find itself confronted with demands for military unions.

LABOR UNIONS

A brief review of the theory of labor movements would safeguard against the formulation, or continuation, of a stylized vision of "unions"—a development that would hardly serve our understanding of the issue at hand. It is a rule that employees do something about the problems brought about by changes in the internal organization of their work place. This action may take the form of informal or spontaneous response, or a formal organization may be created to confront these problems in an organized fashion. Informal organizations created to handle these problems are often unsuccessful when the problems increase in number and complexity, regardless of whether the informal organization is one of workers or managers. It is simply an effort to respond with a modicum of efficiency to unstable or unsatisfactory situations present in a large-scale organization created by technological, economic, or social change.

The types of formal organizations which may arise are determined by the economic, social, technological, or political situations confronting the group, and the goal orientation of the group. These organizations may be craft unions, industrial unions, professional societies, manager associations, foremen clubs, trade associations, and so forth. It is important to note that the emerging formal organization is not necessarily a trade union composed of the labor force of blue-collar workers. It could also be classified simply as a mutual benefit association.

Formal labor organizations, on the other hand, can be characterized by their attempt to seize job control and job ownership. Employing techniques to protect the job is characteristic of the American worker who is concerned with pragmatic goals and not political action. [9] While some unions emphasize economic, other social, and still others political goals, they are all concerned with a single goal of attempting to control external conditions. [10]

Labor unions respond differently to different segments of society, depending on their perceived status and legitimacy. The internal structure of labor unions differs widely within the organized labor movement, reflecting the activities usually found in the work place. There are three types of unions: (1) *business unions,* whose primary function is to increase the economic well-being of the members; (2) *welfare unions,* which seek economic improvements and also increased welfare services—fringe benefits from the employer and broader social security provisions from the government; and (3) *life embracing, or central institutions* in the life of the worker—like the United Mine Workers union. [11]

Ideological unions, on the other hand, which seek social goals broader than the economic improvement of the membership, are not generally found in American society. This type of union usually sees itself as the reforming instrument of an entire society, assured that goals are achievable only through great political involvement. In some countries, the government dominates organized labor. In these settings, the politically aligned left- or right-wing labor associations are part of the government administration. Ideological and government-dominated unions are found in much of Europe.

Some American unions once were similar to those found in Europe; that is, they displayed ideological orientation in the early days of organized labor in this society. However, American labor organizations today are distinctively different from those found in Europe. They are responsive to the conditions present in American society. They are pragmatic, economically powerful, capable of resisting management at the local levels quite effectively, have great internal stability, and object to interference by the church or the state. They have been more successful in resisting Marxist influence than European unions, and less successful in holding out against organized crime. It is also important to note that American unions, unlike most European unions, are seldom constituent parts of a government or political party of any persuasion. Rather, American unions operate as pressure groups in pursuit of the union's pragmatic goals, shifting allegiance to the political part that assists it toward these goals.

Unions work a powerful influence on economic and social conditions in American society disproportionate to their numbers. This control of wages, hours, and working conditions was found to extend into the nonunionized areas thirty years ago. It has been steadily growing ever since. In fact, the struggle between management and unions in the American setting reflects the growing American dilemma of choosing between the work ethic and efficiency on the one hand, and personal independence and equality with a voice in decision making on the other. Regardless of the compassion expressed by managers, workers are hired, fired, moved, promoted, and demoted according to the demands of efficiency and effectiveness. This is the primary function of management. The primary function of unions is to protect the rights of workers as people, and to improve their life style. There is little question that a basis for conflict exists. This conflict will remain as long as the two sides of the issue are identifiable as adversaries to the other's ethic.

It was stated earlier in this paper that European labor movements and organizations are not identical with those found on the American scene. It was also suggested that the military is not unique from many other associations in American society, and that enough similarity exists to warrant the application of generalized social models in our search for understanding the military institution. Public service organizations in particular seem to parallel military entities. It would follow that labor unions in the public sector would be a better guide to the study of American military unions than European military or nonmilitary unions, or private industry trade unions in this country.

During the last decade, the greatest rate of employment growth has been in the public sector, primarily in state and local governments where there was an increase in employees of about 159 percent. [12] During this same period the three unions with the highest growth rate in membership all had a government as their principal employer. The AFGE was the fastest growing union, with a membership increase of 362 percent, compared with the leading private sector union which showed an increase of only 77 percent. The increase is more dramatic as we look to the mid-1970s. More than 800,000 new members joined public sector unions in 1973-1974 which accounts for three-fourths of the total increase in union membership in those years. Clearly, public sector unions display very dynamic growth patterns. Much of the growth in federal employee membership can be attributed to the authorization of collective bargaining by the Kennedy administration in 1962. [13] Authorized collective bargaining in the public sector is a recent development in labor relations.

Although teachers and nonuniformed civil servants constitute the greatest number of public sector union members, police and firefighters are more closely related to military unions and therefore merit our interest. These public sector unions have had a mixed pattern of success in American society, suffering such early setbacks as the unsuccessful strike for wages by firemen in Ithaca, New York, in 1889; some thirty futile walkouts by firefighters across the nation before World War I; and the infamous Boston police strike in 1919 which virtually destroyed police unions in this country for the following twenty five years. Today, however, there are nearly nine hundred policy locals, found in all the states and major cities in the country. Firemen's unions, avoiding violent incidents like those encountered by police, have grown consistently. They are presently nearly twice as large in numbers as police associations.

What is important in the context of this study is the fact that public sector unions in sensitive public safety occupations (police and firefighters) have not been hesitant to use the power of strike to aid their collective bargaining. In the five-year period 1965-1969, fifty-one police strikes and thirty-one strikes by firemen were reported. [14] During the fall of 1975 work stoppages among police and firemen were even higher than in the 1960s. While the prospect that public safety, tax-supported workers would abandon responsible posts and strike may be unthinkable to the private citizen, it can and does happen. Furthermore, job actions short of strikes, such as slowdowns and absenteeism, are probably more numerous than we care to imagine. A twenty-four-hour public sector virus is occasionally found among these uniformed public employees. It has been called "Blue Flu" by opponents of public sector unions.

The question to be asked at this point is: does public sector unionism, particularly the paramilitary organizations of police and firemen, impair government in its attempt to express the will of its citizens in action programs? The answer found by one scholar in a study of fifty local governments across the nation was, "Not much." [15] A later study confirmed these findings concluding:

The unions have narrowed managment discretion, they have fostered the development of management by policy, they have protected employees against arbitrary or inconsistent treatment, and they have shown that management had better begin diverting greater intellectual and organizational resources toward dealing with this new power in their midst. [16]

Can we say the same thing of military unions if they become a reality in the public sector?

MILITARY UNIONS

Alienation is considered to be felt by the worker when an institution leaves an individual's needs unsatisfied or creates problems beyond those a person brought with him to the institution. The agreement to provide work in exchange for the satisfaction of these needs constitutes a "contract" between worker and system. Further, an organization cannot continue to operate unless its membership, or a significant part of it, consents to the authority of its operating system. The consent is given by the work force as long as the institution upholds the contract. In military institutions where consent is in at least some degree "forced," and departure from the contract is not permissible, the membership finds subtle ways of not performing in accordance with the terms of the contract. When the membership feels powerless to bargain with the institution, a mutual benefit association, such as a union, may evolve in order to represent it better. The alternative to an inadequate response by the institution is a continual degradation of performance.

Democracy implies that a group rule themselves either directly or through elected representatives. This is the ideal, and indeed it is not found in most formal and complex organizations. The degree of democracy within an organization is reflective of the style followed by the supporting society, that is, the more democratic the larger society the more democratic its institutions. Military systems have usually been exempt from this lawful model aspect. In such a closed, total institution as the military, self-rule is diminished as one descends the management structure. The democratic decision process is not traditionally found in military organizations. When such a process has been experimentally introduced it has ultimately met with failure and has been discarded. Participation in the military decision process by nonmanagers is a fiction—except in informal structures—which consequently presents a form of psuedo-democracy. There is ample evidence of increased productivity, job satisfaction, and reduced alienation when the work force is allowed such a participatory role. This role has never been permitted in military organizations, however, except in very tentative ways.

In the past, military worker participation in the decision process, a basic characteristic of unionism has been strongly resisted by military management on several grounds. First, it is believed that this would tend to change the structure and identity of the organization. Second, and more important to military (and other) management, it is expected that the function of the institution would be impaired. There is little argument, in light of our experience, that these are justified concerns. Organized labor agrees. However, there are many other possible dimensions of military worker participation in the decision process which can not be as easily set aside.

Workers organize unions in order to increase their bargaining power with employers. [17] This occurs when workers feel their share of the benefits is unfair. Individually, workers can bring little power to bear upon management; collectively, workers assemble power for this bargaining process: they form into unions. Until recently, such action by military workers has been unthinkable in the United States and only marginally endured in Europe—the birthplace of worker organizations.

The survivability of unions depends on the proper identification of the beneficiary. When union benefits shift from the general membership to its leadership the general membership feels that they have been exploited by the leadership, or sold out by it to management. In either case, organizational stability and the viability of the union are in question. If union benefits exceed the means of the organization, the beneficiary is lost as the organization collapses. In the case of civil government unions, the public at large is the employer and the civil servant is the worker. Wilbert Moore has stated that most unions recognize their dependence upon the continued survival of the business. [18] A similar recognition of dependence underlies all conflict relations where there are separate and interdependent functions.

Military unions, then, can be expected to be formed but would be difficult to maintain because of the problems of identifying the true beneficiary and separating the roles of union leadership from those of military leadership. The structure of the military union would not be identified with military managership, at least by the worker group. Introducing an intermediate stratum of leadership is unacceptable to present military organizational management policy. An interesting confrontation would be expected, moreover, if military unions were to become a reality in U.S. organizations. Bureaucratized unions are often ruthlessly efficient. [19] If membership is drawn from such a highly bureaucratic institution as the military, it is expected that, more so than trade unions, they would be especially ruthlessly efficient.

There appear to be four defined regions of interest associated with military unions. These are military management, the Congress, organized labor, and the military worker. Activities in these four regions are better described as a stimulus-response process than a rigorously systematic and comprehensive examination of the problem. The Congress responded vigorously to union interest to survey its membership regarding any future attempt to organize military workers. This response has been in the form of a draft bill to outlaw military unions. According to drafters of the proposed legislation, the military position has not been made clear. Professional associations of some sectors of the military have voiced their resistance to the ideal of military unions. AFL-CIO's American Federation of Government Employees has indicated an interest and intends to recruit uniformed members if the larger membership approves. Little is known about the interest of the fourth region—military workers.

THE UNION POSITION

As stated earlier, alienation from work or the work place appears to be the strongest argument for an organization member to join a union. The rapidly growing interest in military unions, here and in Europe, is testimony that such alienation is believed to be present. Military authorities are maneuvering to resist unionization and organized labor claims unions will be found in American military organizations in the future. We examine now the positions of labor and management on this issue and some impacts on the military if mutual benefit associations—or unions—become a reality.

The American Federation of Government Employees (AFGE), part of the AFL-CIO, in 1976 polled its membership of more than 320,000—over half of whom are Department of Defense civilians—as to whether its constitution should be amended to allow uniformed servicemen to become members. The response was affirmative, and the AFGE constitution was changed. A proposed plan for organizing servicemen was sent to all AFGE locals early in 1977 in order to determine if they do or do not concur with this plan. Results of this referendum are due in October 1977.

Even though the AFGE National Executive Council feels American military unions are not only feasible, but inevitable, the AFGE has not yet decided to organize members of the uniformed military services or admit them to membership in the union. The AFGE feels that a properly managed and represented military union, focused on peacetime activities of living and work conditions outside the combat command channels, could strengthen the military command and control structure. [20] The AFGE is anxious to eliminate the "steward in the foxhole" image and has declared that union recognition would be suspended during war or congressionally declared national defense emergencies. This is in keeping with AFGE policy, which suspended recognition demands for its civilian membership during World War II. However, AFGE would not choose to withdraw its right to strike; in fact, some officials feel a strike by a local cannot be prevented at the national level. [21]

The union intends to represent its uniformed members in first-line grievance matters, including promotions, supervisor ratings, and separation actions. Such representation would be resisted by the military management as an encroachment on command prerogatives. The union would like to see one of its own members sit on promotion boards. AFGE would provide legal support for its members in connection with administrative boards for personnel actions and military justice proceedings. Servicemen are usually not represented by counsel in nonjudicial punishment actions. This would be changed. Legal aid would be made available in more serious cases of special and general court martials. Legislative and policy representation would address the areas of pay, retirement, and fringe benefits. The union says there was little pressure to cut back fringes during the 1960s, but that the "battle of the budget" in competition for the defense dollar began in 1972 with the combatants being the people (servicemen) versus the defense industry. AFGE claims that the defense industry has suffered less than the military worker, and that the outcome begins to describe the classic model of management versus worker.

Membership in military unions would be open to all uniformed servicemen, and AFGE would drive to recruit all ranks from the grade of colonel to private. The union feels that all who enter military service enter into a contract agreement with the employer-government. They allow that officers as well as enlisted men have suffered injustices which could be offset if properly represented by a "third party," or bargaining. AFGE anticipates resistance by the military to this position but feels frustrated because there is no substantial policy statement from the military with which they can argue. It is understood by union officials that eligibility for membership will be determined by the military's definition of the role of *supervisor.* The classic labor definition of supervisor is anyone who has the power to hire, fire, or take disciplinary action. Conceivably, the military could define supervisors to include all ranks down to private, thus reducing potential membership in military unions to about twenty thousand servicemen—each a very short-term member.

AFGE sees military unions as similar to Department of Defense civilians already organized. These organizations would be separate, at the national level, but integrated at the local level. Integration at the local level is considered advisable, at least for the present, in order to provide instruction in the ways of organized labor to the allegedly naive uniformed members. Union locals would be organized in cities or towns adjacent to military installations.

Locals would be organized in units of ten or more members. The shop steward would be elected by the members, ignoring rank, and could be a uniformed serviceman if the local was not integrated with other Defense Department civilians. The bargaining representative is a more difficult position to visualize at this time because of the possible conflict in interest in leadership roles. The bargaining representative must be familiar with the business of the local and general military; ideally a professional active duty or recently retired member is preferred. One can easily see the problem if a military organization's higher ranking officer were also the Union's bargaining representative.

The AFGE is like an industrial union, and considers itself such. However, it desires no input to pre-entry skill certification, such as some trade unions control. It would make recommendations on training; not in the tactical sense, but in work conditions and safety. AFGE feels skill development is the business of management. The AFGE says it does not want to reorganize the military but only to represent uniformed service members who now represent themselves without any real outside help.

THE MILITARY MANAGEMENT POSITION

The military position is that unionization of uniformed members would destroy or seriously disrupt organizational effectiveness, the consequences of which would be failure in combat—the ultimate test of a military organization. The principal objection to military unions is that they would introduce the possibility of dividing loyalty of the membership between the union and the organization by providing a second formal organization parallel with the parent unit. Such duality would disrupt the existing chain of command and possibly impede unquestioning and immediate response to lawful orders. [22]

Secretary of Defense Harold Brown testified before Congress in March 1977 that the changing nature of warfare has consistently decreased the reaction time available to combatants, and that American forces must be quickly and completely responsive to external threats. Collective bargaining as we know it in the civilian process, he suggested, is inconsistent and incompatible with the military need for an unencumbered command and control system. The military views collective bargaining as a form of shared decision making, requiring consultation prior to action. This is unacceptable to command authority. The military has raised the question of the credibility of a unionized military force in the view of potential enemies. There is some concern that a force with a dual control system, such as unionized military, could be considered more vulnerable to attack than one presenting the traditional command control system.

Secretary Brown also put Congress on notice that, in his opinion, hasty legislation aimed at outlawing military unions could run into constitutional difficulties regarding First Amendment issues of protection of speech and association. If one considers that such issues would be tested in the courts, an adverse decision would limit the military's subsequent ability to deal with unions. The military experienced such a setback from prohibitive regulations outlawing union activities. A directive aimed at curtailing recruiting activities of "wild cat" organizers, sarcastically called the "coffee shop order" by opponents, was issued to all military personnel in December 1969. The portion of that directive related to membership in unions was rescinded in December 1976 because it was construed to violate the protection of the First and Fifth Amendments.

The Office of the General Counsel of the Department of Defense is presently engaged in an exhaustive study of the legal complexities of the union question. Apparently, the military will not again be pushed to a hasty policy decision regarding unions. While this may be ultimately beneficial to the military, it is also beneficial to union recruiters. The AFGE claims the military is sitting on the issue and this has given them time to organize a recruiting drive and gather support. The Congress, particularly as a potential sponsor of legislation to outlaw military unions, also has become impatient with the lack of response.

Presently, there are few specific points available to construct a military position on unions. The military fears the chain of command authority will be disrupted, and this will adversely affect the necessary immediate response to lawful orders. Also, the military claims first-line grievances already have a channel of redress—the chain of command. One current policy statement does restrict all members of the Department of Defense from negotiating and bargaining with unions. Dealing with the local union problem, however, has been left to local commanders.

THE IMPACT OF MILITARY UNIONS

The most debilitating impact of a unionized military, according to top military leaders, would be the impairment of combat effectiveness resulting from a disrupted chain of command authority. This consequence is doubtful and probably more characteristic of myth than reality—unless military managers and leaders are also members of the union. The threshold between management and labor is usually narrow, but well defined. Role conflict and attitude consistency will be a severe ordeal for a chain of command incumbent who is also a union member. Also, there is evidence in labor relations literature indicating that such a condition tends to destroy union organization. For example, when the general union membership perceives that the union leadership serves management or itself instead of the membership, internal strength is dissipated through divided efforts to unseat and replace the leadership. Often this splinters the union organization into less effective parts.

The impact on personnel action would, of course, require a major adjustment of policy. AFGE wants union representation on promotion boards, and participation in evaluation and separation review groups. One could expect a union representative to have input in other personnel matters relating to discipline, transfers, hardship duty tours, and those actions affecting member welfare.

Some aspects of the operational role of the armed forces are presently being carried out by union members. Civilian technicians man parts of the navy's operational fleet at sea, and air defense systems around the world depend on unionized nonuniformed workers. This is an observable indicator of a trend toward industrialization of the military and an invitation to military unionism. Impact on tactical operations would be minimal but would be felt nevertheless. For example, preparation for operations requires training, and the union has expressed an interest in reviewing safety control measures for training. This would include weather and other field conditions, equipment, trainer supervision, work hours, food and clothing, and treatment of the trainee.

Another possible impact, which might be overlooked because of its alien (to the military) nature, is the potential politicization of the armed forces. Traditionally, American labor unions do not pursue ideological goals nor are they characterized as radicals. However, the AFL-CIO has usually maintained a very close working relationship with the Democratic party, both at national and local levels. The legal questions of federal employee political involvement will be added to the general questions of constitutionality associated with military unions.

Possible structural changes dominate discussions of the possible impact of unionization. If military union locals can maintain a strong identification with the parent local military organization, a strengthening of primary group relationships might be hypothesized. The importance of primary groups to combat effectiveness has long been recognized. The body of research literature, beginning with the efforts of Stouffer et al. published in the now classical *American Soldier* series of World War II vintage, to the current research of David Segal, does not challenge the importance of these associations, but tracks military groups to measure its presence. [23] Indeed, membership in military union locals could serve to reorient members toward the military community if a military social environment is present to encourage a reinforcement of primary group relationships.

Structural consequences on a level higher than the primary group are also visualized. The appearance and evolution of a union would tend to organize management groups against it. As the struggle progresses, each adversary becomes more unified, with stronger internal relationships.

An increase in the internal cohesion will foster the development of a more enduring group. Action to resist or disallow the formulation of a union among the institutional membership is seen as an open infringement on individual rights. Such action tends to polarize divisions within an organization and produces counter-resistance.

The reserves of all the uniformed services would become more important in the event of military unionization. Unless they, too, were unionized, reserves could be called into service to replace striking active duty personnel. If reservists deferred out of sympathy for their active duty comrades, honoring a "picket line" would increase the power of the union. Also, military organizations have occasionally replaced striking workers in industries considered essential to the national good. A military union could be expected to resist such action if its sympathies were directed toward the striking workers. Recalling that unions are powerful instruments of pressure for legislation favorable to its membership, some control of military legislation would be found in future American military unions. The AFGE has claimed that military management is sacrificing people's benefits in favor of military-oriented industry. As hardware costs increase and reduced military spending is demanded, the continual erosion of fringe benefits, threats against retirement programs, and unfair separation practices are cited by the union as examples of management's solution to this budget conflict. If legislation aimed at improving the lot of the soldier is not forthcoming, union activity—and membership—will grow in the military.

CONCLUSION

There is a high probability that American military unions will be organized in the near future despite the gathering of strong opposition among the management ranks of the executive and legislative branches of government. The changing nature of the military and the external pressure for social change from the larger society will overcome opposition to any form of mutual benefit association of nonmanagement military personnel. The character and nature of American military unions will not be similar to the traditional blue-collar trade unions familiar to American labor, or identical to European military unions. Neither of these types of association provides a good model for understanding U.S. military unions. A better model would be the public sector unions in this country. Insofar as the present methods of military management are concerned, military unions will be disruptive but neither totally dysfunctional nor without benefit to the total military institution. How management copes with these unions, and the unions' response to those efforts, will have significant effect on the future course of civil-military relations in the United States.

NOTES

1. Elting E. Morrison, *Men, Machines, and Modern Times* (Cambridge, Mass.: MIT Press, 1966), pp. 17-44.

2. A. R. Radcliffe-Brown, *A Natural Science of Society* (New York: The Free Press, 1957), pp. 87-88.

3. Thomas S. Kuhn, *The Structure of Scientific Revolutions* (Chicago: University of Chicago Press, 1962), pp. 91-109.

4. Robert Nisbet, *Social Change* (New York: Harper & Row, 1972), pp. 18-19.

5. George C. Homans, *The Human Group* (New York: Harcourt, Brace & World, 1950), pp. 369-414.

6. Donald A. Schon, "The Blindness System" in *The Public Interest,* no. 18 (Winter 1970), pp. 25-38.

7. Lewis Coser, *The Functions of Social Conflict* (New York: The Free Press, 1956), p. 151.

8. Charles C. Moskos, "The Emergent Military: Calling, Profession or Occupation," *Parameters,* vol. 7, no. 1 (1977), pp. 2-9.

9. Selig Perlman, *A Theory of the Labor Movement* (New York: Kelly, 1949).

10. W. E. Moore, "Notes for a General Theory of Labor Organizations," in *Industrial and Labor Relations Review* (April 1960), pp. 389-397.

11. Robert Dubin, *Working Union-Management Relations* (New York: Prentice-Hall, 1958), pp. 209-210.

12. Much of the data and information about public-sector unions was furnished by Edward A. Wilcox, "Unionization of Uniformed Security Forces" (seminar paper, Georgetown University, 1976).

13. Ibid.

14. Jack Stieber, *Public Employee Unionism: Structure, Growth, Policy* (Washington: The Brookings Institution, 1973).

15. David Stanley, *Managing Local Government under Union Pressure* (Washington: The Brookings Institution, 1971).

16. Harvey A. Juris and Peter Feuille, *Police Unionism: Power and Impact in Public Sector Bargaining* (Lexington, Mass: D. C. Heath & Co., 1973).

17. Peter Blau and W. Richard Scott, *Formal Organizations* (San Francisco: Chandler, 1962), pp. 44-49.

18. Wilbert Moore, *Industrial Relations and the Social Order* (New York: Macmillan, 1951), p. 291.

19. Blau and Scott, *Formal Organizations,* pp. 44-49.

20. AFGE National Executive Council Military Committee Memorandum "14/Military," dated March 7, 1977.

21. Interview with G. P. Kenefick, public relations director, AFGE, Washington, March 1977.

22. Interview with Harold Brown, secretary of defense, Washington, March 1977.

23. David R. Segal, a professor of government and sociology at the University of Maryland, is presently engaged in secondary analysis of a national sample of survey data on American serviceman's attitudes toward the military institution.

Chapter Eight
MILITARY UNIONISM IN AMERICA:
RETROSPECT AND PROSPECT [1]

by Alan Ned Sabrosky

IN RETROSPECT: WHY INTEREST IN
AMERICAN MILITARY UNIONS?

From the preceding chapters, we may appreciate more fully than before the complexity of the issue of American military unionism. What is both somewhat surprising and of considerable concern is that the views on military unions are not only diverse, but also markedly polarized. Those who emphasize the importance of individual socioeconomic welfare and civil rights argue that military unions are both constitutional and desirable. Those who give precedence to considerations of the political responsiveness and functional effectiveness of the armed forces take the opposite view. To be sure, academic analyses may find points of commonality on both sides of the issue. Yet little, if any, middle ground mutually acceptable to the contending parties appears in the cases for and against military unions. This absence of a consensus is, perhaps, not unanticipated, but it certainly does not augur well for the final resolution of the issue. In fact, the elements of apparent irreconcilability in the contending arguments for and against military unions may well be indicative of the problems that would affect labor-management relations in a unionized military establishment.

Perhaps the fundamental question to be addressed at this point is *why* interest in military unions seems to be increasing, and what we are to make of that development. Although a number of possible explanations have been suggested, three seem to command wide acceptance. These are based on: (1) general societal trends conducive to prounion sentiment, (2) the advent of the all-volunteer force (AVF), and (3) concern about the continuation of military fringe benefits.

First of all, most agree that general societal trends are moving away from the more traditional concept of "duty, honor, country" in all of its variants, and toward a more self-directed and self-interested system of values. This reduces the willingness of service personnel to accept existing patterns of authority within the military institution, and increases their sense of the incompatibility of institutional restraints with personal freedom of action. Yet the argument that societal trends presage the unionization of the armed forces is far from compelling. "Societal trends" are not inherently positive entities whose maturation should be awaited with either anticipation or resignation. As Gibbon pointed out with depressing clarity in his classic *The Decline and Fall of the Roman Empire, some* aggregate societal trends can undermine an institution, rather than strengthen it. And in fact, many of the existing trends in American society do not seem particularly well suited to the requirements of disciplined cohesion essential to the armed forces of a nation with global responsibilities. Needless to say, such trends should be countered within the military institution, if they cannot be corrected outside of it.

Second, a clear linkage is made between the creation of the all-volunteer force and the rise of substantial interest in military unionism. The decision to require the armed forces to compete on the labor market for the necessary numbers of recruits produced a job-orientation within the military that is conducive to prounion sentiment, particularly among first-term personnel. Once military service was defined in occupational rather than professional terms, the presumption of institutional uniqueness was weakened, and with it many of the arguments against unionization. [2] Nevertheless, while the movement to an all-volunteer force certainly stimulated the development of the preconditions for unionization, all-volunteer forces are not inherently union-prone. In fact, all of the countries in which some form of military unions exists also have some form of conscription, while nations which rely entirely on volunteers to meet the manpower needs of their armed forces do not have military unions. Several European military unions do include professional military personnel, of course, and some are even restricted to career servicemen. Yet by and large, the most active and vocal unions have been seen as means by which conscripts could improve their position and welfare in ways that the military establishment would not otherwise allow. [3]

Finally, it is certainly true that the actual or perceived erosion of some collateral military benefits, and the threatened erosion of others, have raised concern among many military careerists about a wide range of individual, welfare-related issues. This, in turn, has made them more willing to consider alternative ways of ensuring that existing benefits would be retained, if not expanded. But it also should be recognized that the erosion of benefits has not been so great as some have believed to be the case. This is particularly apparent when seen in light of the significantly better pay scales now enjoyed by military personnel relative to conditions of a decade age. [4] Collateral benefits once were seen as a way of compensating service personnel for the significant disparity which existed between military and civilian wages. With comparability between those wages more nearly approached, the objective need for some of the collateral benefits ought to have decreased. This is not the case, at least in the eyes of many career military personnel. And the fact that they see this to be a major issue may say more about the changing values and sense of priorities of some career military personnel than it does about the alleged sense of deprivation they may feel.

Whatever their validity, the combined effect of these (and other) factors has been to increase the attractiveness of military unions to service personnel, regardless of how the general population might view such unions. Preliminary studies of military personnel have found that a majority of those surveyed either support or are uncertain about the desirability of military unionization. A plurality of all respondents and a majority of commissioned officers remain opposed to military unions. Yet a majority of both commissioned and enlisted respondents agreed that military unions would increase the economic well-being of those in the armed services. [5] Thus, a continuation of present societal trends in the context of an all-volunteer force in which collateral benefits were threatened or reduced could be expected to increase support for unions among military personnel. This does not mean that military unions are inevitable in America, despite claims to that effect in some circles. It does suggest, however, that the possibility that the U.S. armed forces might be unionized is all too likely to increase in coming years.

RELEVANT ANALOGIES: A CRITICAL APPRAISAL

Since American military unions do not now exist, we must look elsewhere for evidence that might apply to the performance of such unions in this country. At first glance, it would seem that such evidence would be readily obtainable from studies of both Western European military unions and the union movement in the United States, especially in the public sector. Yet many analysts entertain at least some reservations about their relevance as sources of insights into whatever American military unions might come to pass.

This is particularly apparent in the case of the Western European military unions. [6] In fact, one is struck by (1) the amount of effort that is given to deprecating the relevance of the Western European experience with military unions, and (2) the selectivity employed by those who *do* attempt to draw on that experience in their arguments for or against American military unions. It is generally argued, for example, that the differences between the European and the American union movements seriously weaken (if not invalidate) the values of Western European analogues to American military unionism. Such an approach, however, seems unwarranted. American military unions certainly would have at least some of the organizational objectives and interests of their European counterparts. Unions in any country exist in part for the purpose of improving the socioeconomic welfare of their members. They may do more than that, of course, and they may perform even their minimum functions more or less efficiently. The fact that our military unions would partake of the traditions of American rather than European unionism could not be discounted entirely. But one simply cannot say that an organization in this country will be fundamentally different from a comparable organization in another country.

It must be conceded, of course, that European unions have tended to be more politicized and ideologically motivated than their more pragmatic, "bread-and-butter" American counterparts. Yet the fact that they have been different in the past does not mean that they will remain so indefinitely. Unionization is an evolutionary process, not a static condition. Institutions and movements may start from different places, but it does not follow that they will pursue inexorably different paths thereafter. Convergence may occur, with one movement adopting the characteristics of the other, or some synthesis of the two may evolve.

In this context, it seems that American unionism in general, and public sector unions in particular, are becoming more like their European counterparts in practice than once was the case. Public sector unions *by definition* deal with issues that have broader social and political implications than do questions of working conditions and retirement benefits. [7] That they should act on issues not directly related to the more conventional "work place, wages, and grievances" concerns of private sector trade unions, therefore, ought not to be surprising. Thus, the European union movement in general, and European military unions in particular, may not reflect either the American union movement at the present time, or even the type of military union which might evolve from that movement. But it could well suggest what that movement and that military union might become at some point in the future.

It is certainly true that the national defense establishment of the United States has a very different set of missions than is the case with the defense establishments of the several Western European countries, whether or not they have military unions. Yet the missions of certain parts of those military establishments are not that different. At the strategic level, to be sure, the requirements levied on the American forces are more extensive and more demanding than those placed on the Western European armed forces. Questions of credibility of response, efficacy of command and control, and the reliability of the strategic deterrent force as they might be affected by unionization cannot be answered with any degree of certainty from the European experience. [8] Yet there exists much greater compar-

146

ability with respect to the missions of Western European and American general purpose forces. Should a war occur in Central Europe, for example, the unionized *Bundeswehr* and the currently nonunionized U.S. Seventh Army would be confronted with quite similar tasks. Thus, whatever institutional strengths or weaknesses in a *Bundeswehr* formation might be attributable to unionization would likely appear in an equivalent American organization.

To assess those strengths and weaknesses requires a comprehensive assessment of the diverse types of Western European military unions. Yet it is here that the second difficulty—that of selectivity on the part of those who *do* choose to use Western European military unions as an analogy— becomes important. There exist a number of scholarly and professional studies of European military unions, of course. Yet in political circles, both civilian and military, a less demanding and less critical approach seems evident. That is, those who *do* see some relevance in the European experience with military unionism all too often focus on the Dutch and West German military associations. Supporters of American military unions look at both countries, emphasizing the "democratizing" influence of military unions in the Netherlands and the superior quality of the heavily unionized *Bundeswehr*. [9] Opponents of military unions in the U.S. also look at the Dutch armed forces, but as an example of what a military establishment ought *not* to become.

Although neither the Dutch nor the West German military associations are unions "[in] the strictest sense" [10], Bonn's large, efficient, and extensively unionized military establishment seems particularly atypical. The greatest problems with unions are presumed to come from those that are restricted to junior enlisted personnel, and particularly conscripts. Yet the West German unions include all ranks of enlisted and commissioned personnel within the same organization. At the very least, unions that include in their membership general staff colonels and regular army lieutenant generals might have a certain leavening that less all-inclusive unions would not. Perhaps the most important consideration, however, is that the labor-management relationship in West German society simply is not analogous to that which exists in the United States, or even in the rest of Western Europe. In the FRG, labor and management cooperate to a significant degree, and that cooperation facilitates the resolution of controversies that might cause a strike or job action in other countries. It would be surprising if a similar tradition had not extended into the military unions themselves. In fact, the principal West German military union (the DBwV) has been described accurately even by advocates of military unionization as a "company union." [11]

147

On balance, the West German military unions are sufficiently different from their European counterparts and what might be expected to arise in the United States that they are a dubious analogy at best. The Dutch military unions, however, appear much closer to the European norm. They also reflect concerns that would be likely to appear regarding the American military if this country's armed forces were to be unionized. To be sure, the real value of military forces such as those of the Netherlands is difficult to evaluate. The unkempt appearance of the Dutch soldiery certainly does not recommend military unionism to parade-ground enthusiasts. Yet the Israeli Defense Force (perhaps an exception) also takes a somewhat cavalier approach to certain elements of standard military protocol without adversely affecting its combat ability.

The problem with the unionized Dutch armed forces, however, is one of credibility. Even if they *are* still competent, their appearance and behavior are such that neither their allies nor their adversaries truly seem to believe it. Habits acquired in peacetime are not easily discarded at will once a war begins, and the habits displayed by the Dutch forces simply are not indicative of the qualities needed to maintain a high level of disciplined competence in war. Such appearances may be deceiving, but when they occur in a military establishment they may contribute to miscalculations on *both* sides that lead to an undesired war.

If the case could be made that an American military union would be like a German military union, then even present opponents of military unions might be inclined to embrace the concept. Unfortunately for the proponents of military unionization, however, that is unlikely to be the case. It is all too likely that the West German military unions are the exception, rather than the rule. Further, the uncertainties raised by the Dutch military unions neither argue for the unionization of the U.S. armed forces, nor augur well for the consequences of their unionization if it should occur.

Whatever else they might be, of course, the American military unions would partake of the characteristics of the union movement in this country. There are clearly fewer reservations about the relevance of American unionism to a study of U.S. military unionization than there are with respect to the European military unions. As Professor Wyatt points out in Chapter Seven, for example, organizations share a number of characteristics that permit analogies to be drawn, at least if reasonable caution is exercised. When both military and nonmilitary institutions are industrialized and bureaucratic entities arising within the same political culture, the analogies may hold particularly well. Thus, the performance of unions in a corporate setting might not be all that different from their performance in a military setting.

In addition, it is likely that whatever union would actually organize the military would also include civilian members. This would certainly be the case with the American Federation of Government Employees, the National Association of Government Employees, the Association of Civilian Technicians, and most of the other groups that are, or have been, interested in setting up military unions. (In fact, only the more radical groups such as the Enlisted Peoples' Organizing Committee might enroll an almost exclusively military membership, although even that is not certain.) This amalgamation of military and civilian personnel would undermine the allegedly unique character of an American military union in the same way as the emphasis on the military as an occupation undermined the presumably unique character of the military institution.

Finally, armed public security forces at all levels of government share a number of functional similarities. Perhaps the most notable of these is the possession of a monopoly on the legitimate use of force within their respective jurisdictions. This suggests that *unions* of their personnel could also share a number of behavioral similarities. Thus, a study of police unions could provide insights into what we might expect from military unions, at least with respect to their willingness to adhere to contractual limitations on union behavior. Regrettably, the mixed record of police unions on this point is not reassuring. Some have acted with restraint and moderation. Others, however, have acted contrary to the public interest by engaging in "job actions" to gain additional bargaining power during contract negotiations. Even the slightest possibility that a military union would do likewise would be politically and militarily intolerable.

THE IMPACT OF UNIONIZATION ON THE U.S. MILITARY

Barring some unanticipated development, it is distinctly possible that the U.S. military will be unionized if current manpower levels are maintained in the present recruiting environment. The principal question to be answered, therefore, is: *What would military unions mean for America?* Future developments, of course, may produce a situation very different from that which we can anticipate at this time. What are seen to be relevant analogies at present may turn out to have been entirely mistaken, while others that were dismissed out of hand may be seen in retrospect to have been closer to the mark. Yet the evidence seems sufficiently clear in a sufficiently large number of cases to permit several preliminary conclusions to be drawn with a fairly high degree of confidence.

What must be recognized, first of all, is that when we speak of American military unions, we are talking about the unionization of all of the armed services. One union or many, organized by rank or open to all service personnel, restricted to military personnel or open to civilians as well, either the American military will be unionized *in toto* or not at all. The partial unionization of the armed forces is simply too unworkable, militarily and politically speaking, to be a viable course of action. Moreover, it does seem that the organization which took the lead in unionizing the military could make a difference, at least in the short term. Military personnel enrolled in the relatively moderate AFGE, for example, would be subject to a different set of union constraints and predispositions than if the Enlisted Peoples' Organizing Committee won out. In the long term, however, certain general consequences are likely to follow the unionization of the armed forces by *any* organization. These general consequences are obviously of the most immediate interest.

The first point that must be acknowledged is that a number of gains are registered for unionized workers in the case of both European military unions and American private and public sector unions. Unionization does improve the economic well-being of union members, relative to that of workers in comparable occupations who are not unionized. Pay increases more rapidly, and benefits are improved and guaranteed more securely, than is the case in nonunionized occupations. All of these gains probably would appear in a unionized American military establishment.

In addition, grievance procedures would be expanded and diversified. This would give unionized military personnel alternate and probably more effective means of rectifying intentional or unintentional institutional abuses than currently exists in the defense establishment. Unionized military personnel would achieve an added measure of job security. The "reduction in force" (R. I. F.) measures which are used to reduce the number of personnel in specific grades and occupational specialties would be moderated, and would become the subject of negotiation and arbitration. It would be more difficult to give less than honorable discharges. Unionization also would produce a more differentiated managerial structure. That structure probably would stop short of codetermination (shared direction of affairs by officials of both labor and management). It would, however, still involve union officials from shop stewards to the national union president(s) and governing council(s) in a wide range of decison areas now reserved solely to military management.

These certain effects of the unionization of the U.S. military services, as well as the society at large. The first direct effect of military unionization is that manpower costs would increase sharply over time, both in the absolute and in the proportion to what would exist in the defense budget of a nonunionized American defense establishment of the same size. If unions do nothing else well, they do raise wages and increase benefits, including retirement compensation, for their members. Achieving these essential union goals would confront any Administration with a particularly demanding decision. To maintain current manpower levels without cutting sharply into other appropriations categories (e.g., operations and maintenance), substantial increases in defense outlays would have to be accepted. If defense outlays were not to increase significantly, then extensive reductions would be required in manpower levels, major appropriations categories other than manpower-related expenditures, or both. It would be very difficult, however, to reduce manpower levels in a unionized military. Opposing reductions in the size of the workforce, after all, has a very high priority in most unions. [12] To hold down defense outlays in a unionized defense establishment, therefore, extensive cutbacks would have to be made in other appropriations categories—probably operations and maintenance or procurement, as they would be the largest remaining categories. *Thus, the unionization of the U.S. armed forces would entail either higher defense costs or a certain reduction in operational capabilities, if not both.*

The second consequence of unionization is that the exercise of direct managerial authority would be inhibited at all levels. Unit leaders of any rank will be subject to greater constraints on their behavior than would otherwise exist in areas once considered the purview of the unit commander. Some interface of the "official" and "union" chains of command necessarily would occur as a consequence of union participation in *any* decision now made solely by the military hierarchy. To presume that a blurring of command responsibilities could be restricted to questions of individual welfare, pay and promotions, and peacetime grievance procedures seems unwarranted. On the contrary: many of the decisions that have the greatest effect on individual servicemen are operational decisions made in wartime. As we noted earlier, it is unwarranted to presume that habits acquired in peacetime service would be discarded without hesitation at the onset of war or national emergency, *even if the union leadership directed that to happen.* Human beings simply do not work that way, even in the most controlled societies.

Third, no matter how restricted the initial scope of a union's charter, its powers eventually would expand to include collective bargaining and, ultimately, either the right or the *de facto* power to conduct strikes or job actions to press home its demands. [13] During his confirmation hearings, Secretary of Labor Ray Marshall indicated that he favored "some form of union representation for the armed forces—but without the right to strike." [14] Such a position, however, is untenable. Without the fact or the threat of strike, a union has no way to obtain from management what management is unwilling to give of its own volition. In fact, the best time for a union to press home its demands is when management has the greatest need of union members' services—namely, during a crisis or national emergency, in the case of military unions.

It is all too obvious that the step from low-key unionism to a more aggressive variety is one that will be taken by any union leadership unwilling to stagnate. [15] Military unions, like their police union predecessors, might not initially have the power to strike or engage in "job actions." Yet unless one believes that a military union will somehow be unique, that power will come with time. In such circumstances, neither the government nor the nation will have any effective recourse to deal with a strike or job action by those on whom the authority of the government ultimately depends. [16] There is, I would argue, an "iron law" of public policy applicable here: *No society can tolerate shared authority over armed personnel responsible for the maintenance of public safety without risking the very survival of the constitutional order.* The unionization of the armed forces would create such an environment of shared authority.

Fourth, there is no clear indication that military unionization either enhances or undermines the functional effectiveness of the armed forces, at least during peacetime. Professors Krendel and Wyatt, for example, concluded in their chapters that official fears of an erosion in the combat effectiveness of a unionized military probably were overdrawn. And on reflection, this may be true with respect to the technical proficiency of individual service personnel. Yet armed forces are more than simple aggregations of technically competent individuals. Disciplined organization and unit proficiency also are essential, and it is these aspects of the military that unionization would be likely to affect adversely. At the very least, the adversary relationship inherent in most labor-management situations probably would be intensified by unionization, thereby undermining that *esprit de corps* essential to success in war. The fact that noncommissioned officers and enlisted personnel in general seem nearly twice as willing as officers to support military unions [17] suggests the evolution of an adversary relationship in a unionized U.S. military that could not be beneficial to the long-term institutional cohesion of the armed forces.

Fifth, and finally, unionization would prompt the eventual politicization of the armed forces. All except the strongest advocates of military unions appear to express some concern about the possible impact of unionization on the political responsiveness of the military. There is, of course, little doubt that a politicized defense establishment is undesirable. As one writer concluded, "A politicized, class-conscious military, taught to go out and wrest resources from the public, its employer, would be a danger to our democracy." [18] No one would argue that the present military establishment is divorced from the mainstream of practical politics in Washington, *insofar as they bear on the institutional interests of the military itself.* What would make a unionized military establishment politicized would be its linkage to a larger, more diversified public or private sector union. This would bring the added bargaining power of the union's military members into the balance on a wide range of issues that would not necessarily bear directly on the concerns of the military itself. Eventually, this would call into question the reliability of the military in any conflict situation, foreign or domestic, not favored by the union leadership. Such a development certainly is not in our national interest.

RESPONSE TO THE CHALLENGE OF MILITARY UNIONS

For those to whom the maintenance of an effective national defense is paramount, the immediate question is how the challenge of military unionism might best be met. One way of dealing with this problem is to try and remove the incentives for unionization. The occupational image associated with the all-volunteer force and the feared loss of collateral military benefits are perhaps the principal stimuli to pro-union sentiment in the services. The latter factor is theoretically the most manageable: an Administration could decide not to reduce benefits, and even increase them. Yet such an approach is both unwise and unlikely to be effective. It is unwise because it amounts to an attempt to bribe career military personnel not to unionize, thereby reducing them implicitly to the status of mercenaries. The precedent this would set is not pleasant to contemplate. It is unlikely to be effective because trying to beat a union on its own preferred ground— that is, the ability to get greater concessions from management than management is willing to give—is fruitless. At the very least, a union can always promise to make management give more than management *can* give without eroding institutional viability.

An attempt to move away from the occupational image now characterizing the military is also unlikely to be successful in the present recruiting environment. This is due to the difficulty of implementing any other model of service while still competing for sufficient recruits to meet existing manpower needs in a society whose values are not conducive to service in the armed forces. Nor would a return to conscription (or anything approximating it) necessarily reduce the primacy of the occupational model and the attendant prounion sentiment. In fact, either a return to conscription or an attempt to institute some form of compulsory national service (which is closer to outright conscription than some acknowledge) probably would hasten the unionization of the military, even if either course of action was politically feasible. Dissatisfied conscripts or "compulsory national servicepeople" could well be far more interested in unionization than those

153

volunteers who, for whatever reason, chose to enter the service. If that were coupled with the continued dissatisfaction of long-term service personnel, a return to conscription or its equivalent could give union advocates the majority they would need.

If the incentives for unionization within the military cannot easily be removed, one possible recourse is to legislate against military unions. This approach, as we have seen, is being attempted. [19] A number of officials, however, including President Carter, Secretary of Defense Harold Brown, and Navy Secretary W. Graham Claytor, Jr., have expressed reservations about the constitutionality of legislation prohibiting the unionization of the U.S. military. And in fact, the constitutional question clearly is seen by many to be the crux of the matter. It is a foregone conclusion that the passage of any legislation either restricting or endorsing military unions in any shape or form, or even a vote by service personnel to unionize in the absence of such legislation, will be tested in the courts. In the past, the Supreme Court in particular has tended to grant military personnel civil rights separate from, but not quite equal to, those enjoyed by the civil society at large. It also seems that the present Court probably would continue that practice and deny the right of any organization to unionize military personnel, although this is certainly open to question.

In terms of abstract ethics, of course, this *de facto* segregation of the military from the civil society is unconscionable in a political democracy that, as the advocates of military unions put it, prides itself on its citizen soldiers. Yet this practice should not be surprising. Perhaps only garrison states whose militarized societies exist for the purpose of fighting, or peripheral states whose civilianized military establishments simply are not expected to have to fight, can afford to grant their soldiery the same civil rights and individual liberties accorded to the rest of their citizens. In all other states, the requirements levied on the armed forces differ so greatly from the obligations expected of the civil society that to grant military personnel the same latitude as civilians would likely result in a defense establishment that could not protect, and might well threaten, the society it was supposed to guard.

The key issue here, however, may not be the constitutionality of such legislation, but rather its *enforceability*. A recent report on the effectiveness of anti-union legislation at state and local levels, for example, concluded that "laws have slowed or hindered union organization (of public employees), but have not been able to prevent it." [20] In the case of legislation against military unions, these difficulties would be increased. For the military to be unionized, after all, would require the support of a majority of at least one service, and a plurality of the entire defense establishment.

Precisely how one would enforce legislation prohibiting unionization against the wishes of a military whose personnel were determined to unionize is not clear. Appeals to supporters of police unions for restraint in the name of "public welfare" have not been well received by them. There is little reason to think that supporters of a military union would respond differently.

This suggests that attempting to enforce anti-union legislation in such a situation could prompt a constitutional confrontation that would not be in anyone's interest. The question, then, ought not to be whether legislation prohibiting the unionization of the U.S. military is constitutional. It is how quickly such legislation can be passed and brought before the Supreme Court for affirmation of its constitutionality. The sooner those steps are taken, the less widespread and less entrenched pro-union sentiment will be in the military, and the more likely it is that such legislation would be enforceable.

On the other hand, it must be recognized that it may be too late for such legislation to be implemented even if it were passed by Congress, signed into law by the President, and affirmed by the Supreme Court. If pro-union sentiment became sufficiently strong in the armed forces, neither the passage of legislation prohibiting military unions nor the affirmation of the constitutionality of such legislation would suffice to stave off the unionization of the U.S. military. At best, the challenge of military unionization might only be postponed.

If this should be the case, then there are only three remaining ways of dealing with the situation. The first is simply to accept the unionization of the military by whatever groups can gain the necessary support from within the services. This alternative, however, is unappealing. It is quite possible that unionization would enhance the welfare of individual service personnel, as well as democratizing the armed forces to a greater extent than would otherwise be possible. Yet it is certain that the political and military liabilities that would be incurred as a result of the unionization of the armed forces would be undesirable. To let the union movement take its course in the military risks conceding the numbers, dues, and bargaining power of a two million member defense establishment to an increasingly active, and potentially activist, labor organization. Such a development would, in my opinion, take unwarranted liberties with our national security and our constitutional process.

The second option, therefore, would attempt to reduce the risk that a unionized military would become a highly politicized adversary of its management, the Federal Government. It entails a decision to steal a march on the military union movement by creating a *de facto* "company union" based on an expansion and amalgamation of the existing professional service associations. Such a "general military association" would be all-inclusive in membership in order to reduce the sense of "we-they" all too characteristic of most labor-management relationships. Whenever possible, the same individuals should hold comparable positions in the union and the military hierarchies. At the very least, gross discrepancies between military rank and union office ought not to occur. Such an association certainly would be preferable to a more conventional union affiliate, however difficult it would be to put it together. Yet encouraging the creation of even an initially supportive "company union" in the military would be a high-risk venture. Such an association, too, could well evolve into a more activist organization, much as has occurred with the AFGE and the various "policemen's benevolent associations." Thus, forming a company union could be only a way of delaying an eventual union-management confrontation in the military.

The third course of action rejects the desirability of any military union, whatever its initial relationship with the defense establishment. It reflects a judgment that the unionization of the armed forces can only be prevented by reducing military manpower requirements significantly below current levels. This would essentially entail major reductions in the existing general purpose ground forces, coupled with a lengthening of the initial term of service. The resulting decrease in the need for recruits would allow the services to access fewer numbers of higher-quality recruits for longer enlistments than is now possible. Properly managed, this approach could result in a smaller but more professional military that is adequately compensated *and* adequately motivated for military service, as well as adequate for the legitimate needs of national defense. [21] Such a military would hardly constitute a receptive audience for advocates of military unions.

CONCLUSION

In sum, what must be understood is that any case for military unionization rests on the contentions that military unions would be nonpartisan, apolitical, quiescent during periods of national emergency, and totally unwilling to employ their most effective instrument—the strike—in order to lend weight to their demands. Such contentions, it seems to me, are not justified. There is no sound reason to assume that military unions would exercise indefinitely a degree of politically neutral self-restraint and self-denial unparalleled in the history of the union movement. Certainly, little in the performance to date of American public sector unions substantiates such an assumption. To rely on a military union *not* to act like a union over the long term is, in my opinion, fundamentally unwise. Unions have a proper, well-earned place in American society, but that place should not encompass the armed forces.

1. Part of the discussion in this chapter appeared in the author's "Unionization and the U.S. Military: A Conference Report," *Orbis* 21, no. 2 (Summer 1977).

2. For a thoughtful discussion of differing orientations toward military service, see Charles C. Moskos, Jr., "The All Volunteer Military: Calling, Profession, or Occupation?" *Parameters* 7, no. 1 (1977). It should be noted, however, that military service rarely was defined as a "calling" by enlisted personnel. Their choice usually was limited to viewing the military as either an "occupation" or a "profession." This distinction should be noted when considering measures to correct prounion sentiment among enlisted personnel.

3. Professor Ezra S. Krendel emphasized this point in his presentation at the Foreign Policy Research Institute Executive Conference on Unionization and the U.S. Military, Philadelphia, Pa., April 22, 1977.

4. See, for example, Paul N. Schratz, "The Military Union Card," *United States Naval Institute Proceedings* (June 1977), pp. 27-29.

5. See T. Roger Manley, C. W. McNichols, and G. C. S. Young, "Attitudes of Active Duty Air Force Personnel Toward Military Unionization," *Armed Forces and Society* 3, no. 4 (Summer 1977), and a comparison of their findings with a survey of army personnel in James K. McCollum and Jerald F. Robinson, A Study of Active Army Attitudes toward Unionization" (paper presented at the 39th Military Operations Research Society Symposium, USNA, Annapolis, Md., June 28-30, 1977), esp. pp. 12-13. The evidence *is* limited, but the similarities in the findings of surveys of two different services are striking.

6. In addition to the chapter on European military unions in this book, see also Gerald F. Perselay, "The Western European Military Model" (paper presented at the 39th Military Operations Research Society Symposium, USNA, Annapolis, Md., June 28-30, 1977), esp. pp. 5-8.

7. The U.S. Supreme Court recently acknowledged this point. Writing for the majority of the Court, Mr. Justice Stewart concluded that "There can be no quarrel with the truism that because public employee unions attempt to influence governmental policy-making, their activities and the view of members who disagree with them may be properly termed political." *Abood v. Detroit Board of Education,* 97 S. Ct. 1782, 1797 (1977).

8. Professor Edward Bernard Glick of Temple University has given particular emphasis to the importance of the "superpower factor" in assessing the implications of military unionism in the United States.

9. See, for example, David E. Cortright, "Unions and Democracy," *AEI Defense Review,* no. 1 (1977), esp. pp. 7-8.

10. See, for example, Perselay, "Western European Military Model," p. 8.

11. Cortright, "Unions and Democracy," p. 8. The influence of cultural variations, of course, is imprecisely understood. Yet it might be noted that the Germans have shown themselves to be rather good at fielding efficient armies under a variety of different regimes and situations. That the unionized *Bundeswehr* was

still highly proficient might therefore be due to the fact that it was German rather than that it was unionized.

12.   Needless to say, any attempt to reduce manpower levels in a unionized U.S. defense establishment would almost certainly lead to a major rift between military management and the union leadership.

13.   Even prounion spokesmen acknowledge trends toward more assertive public sector unionization in the United States, and expanding powers for European military unions. See, for example, Cortright, "Unions and Democracy," pp. 5-7.

14.   Quoted in *U.S. News and World Report,* 14 February 1977, p. 8.

15.   The American Federation of Government Employees, for example, initially included a no-strike provision in its charter. That self-imposed restraint was discarded at the AFGE's convention in 1976—the same convention at which the AFGE charter was amended to permit enrollment of military personnel—when the union's membership voted to authorize strikes or "job actions."

16.   Harry E. Eccles, "Military Unionization: The Central Issues," *Naval War College Review* 30, no. 1 (Summer 1977), p. 24. It should be noted that unionized police forces are tolerated in some sectors only because of the certainty that, if necessary, striking police could be replaced by either the National Guard or the regular armed forces. If the National Guard and the armed forces were themselves unionized, neither that certainty nor that option would exist.

17.   McCollum and Robinson, "Active Army Attitudes toward Unionization," p. 13.

18.   Charles L. Parnell, "Should Military Unionization Be Permitted?" *United States Naval Institute Proceedings,* (July 1977), p. 24.

19.   On August 18, 1977, for example, the Senate Armed Services Committee reported out legislation that would prohibit both military unions and the unionization of civilians employed by the armed forces. (*Washington Post,* August 28, 1977).

20.   Report by Kraemer Associates, Inc., cited in Vernon Guidrey, "Collective Bargaining Is Called 'Distinct Possiblity' for Military," *Washington Star,* 15 February 1977.

21.   This proposal is developed at length in my *Defense Manpower Policy: A Critical Reappraisal* (Philadelphia, Pa.: Foreign Policy Research Institute, Monograph No. 22, 1977).

APPENDIX A

CONFERENCE AGENDA

Welcome and Opening Remarks

The Honorable William R. Kintner, President
    Foreign Policy Research Institute

Panel I: Examining the Issues in Military Unionism

Moderator: Alan Ned Sabrosky
             Foreign Policy Research Institute

Papers: "Issues in Military Unionization"
             (Col. William J. Taylor, Jr., U.S. Military Academy)

             "The Case for Military Unionization"
             (Col. Gene Phillips, USA, Ret.)

             "The Case Against Military Unionization"
             (Theodore L. Humes, Public Service Research Council)

Discussants: Edward Bernard Glick, Temple University
             David R. Segal, University of Maryland

Panel II: Record and Implications of Military Unionism

Moderator: Richard E. Bissell
             Foreign Policy Research Institute

Papers: "Military Unionism Abroad"
             (Ezra S. Krendel, Wharton School, University of
             Pennsylvania)

             "American Military Unions"
             (Thomas C. Wyatt, George Mason University of Virginia)

Discussants: David Y. Denholm, Public Service
                Research Council

             Virgel Miller, American Federation of
                Government Employees

Concluding Remarks

The Honorable William R. Kintner, President
    Foreign Policy Research Institute

95TH CONGRESS
1ST SESSION

S. 274

IN THE SENATE OF THE UNITED STATES

JANUARY 18, 1977

Mr. THURMOND (for himself, Mr. ALLEN, Mr. BAKER, Mr. BARTLETT, Mr. BELL-MON, Mr. BENTSEN, Mr. HARRY F. BYRD, JR., Mr. CHILES, Mr. CURTIS, Mr. DANFORTH, Mr. DOLE, Mr. DOMENICI, Mr. EASTLAND, Mr. GARN, Mr. GOLDWATER, Mr. HANSEN, Mr. HATCH, Mr. HAYAKAWA, Mr. HELMS, Mr. HOLLINGS, Mr. LAXALT, Mr. LUGAR, Mr. McCLELLAN, Mr. McCLURE, Mr. MORGAN, Mr. NUNN, Mr. SCHMITT, Mr. SCOTT, Mr. STEVENS, Mr. STONE, Mr. TALMADGE, Mr. TOWER, Mr. WALLOP, Mr. YOUNG, and Mr. ZORINSKY) introduced the following bill; which was read twice and referred to the Committee on Armed Services

---

A BILL

To amend chapter 49 of title 10, United States Code, to prohibit union organization in the armed forces, and for other purposes.

1   *Be it enacted by the Senate and House of Representa-*
2   *tives of the United States of America in Congress assembled,*
3   That (a) chapter 49 of title 10, United States Code, is
4   amended by adding at the end thereof a new section as
5   follows:
6   **"§ 975. Union organizing and membership prohibited**
7   "(a) As used in this section—

II

161

1   " (1) 'Member of the armed forces' means a mem-

2   ber of the armed forces who is (A) serving on active

3   duty, (B) a member of a Reserve component, or (C)

4   in a retired status.

5   " (2) 'Labor organization' means any organization

6   of any kind in which employees (including members

7   of the armed forces) participate and which exists for

8   the purpose, in whole or in part, of dealing with em-

9   ployers concerning conditions of work. Such term does

10   not include any fraternal or professional organization

11   unless such organization supports, advocates, or asserts

12   the right of employees of the Government of the United

13   States or members of the armed forces to strike against

14   the Government of the United States.

15   " (3) 'Employer' includes the United States

16   Government.

17   " (b) It shall be unlawful for any individual, group,

18 association, organization, or other entity to enroll any mem-

19 ber of the armed forces in, or to solicit or otherwise en-

20 courage any member of the armed forces to join, any labor

21 organization.

22   " (c) (1) It shall be unlawful for any member of the

23 armed forces to be a member of or to solicit or to otherwise

24 encourage any other member of the armed forces to join

25 any labor organization.

26   " (2) It shall be unlawful for any member of the armed

1 forces to actively support any activity of any labor organiza-
2 tion if such activity (1) is a protest against, is intended to
3 focus public attention on, or is for the purpose of bringing
4 about changes in, the working conditions of members of the
5 armed forces, or (2) supports, advocates, or asserts the
6 right of members of the armed forces to join or be repre-
7 sented by labor organizations.

8 "(d) The provisions of subsections (b) and (c) shall
9 not apply in any case in which any individual, group, associ-
10 ation, organization, or other entity enrolls any member of
11 the armed forces in, or solicits or otherwise encourages any
12 member of the armed forces to join, any labor organization,
13 or in any case in which a member of the armed forces joins
14 a labor organization or solicits or otherwise encourages an-
15 other member of the armed forces to join a labor organiza-
16 tion if the labor organization concerned does not represent,
17 or purport or attempt to represent, the interests of members
18 of the armed forces in any dealings or negotiations, or in
19 any attempt to deal or negotiate, with the Government of
20 the United States and does not advocate or assert the right
21 of members of the armed forces to strike against the Govern-
22 ment of the United States.

23 "(e) (1) Any individual violating subsection (b) or
24 (c) shall be punished by imprisonment of not more than
25 five years.

1   " (2) Any labor organization guilty of violating sub-

2 section (b) shall be punished by a fine of not less than

3 $25,000 or more than $50,000.".

4   (b) The table of sections at the beginning of chapter

5 49 of title 10, United States Code, is amended by adding

6 at the end thereof the following:

"975. Union organizing and membership prohibited.".

95TH CONGRESS
1ST SESSION

S. 274

A BILL

To amend chapter 49 of title 10, United States Code, to prohibit union organization in the armed forces, and for other purposes.

By Mr. THURMOND, Mr. ALLEN, Mr. BAKER, Mr. BARTLETT, Mr. BELLMON, Mr. BENTSEN, Mr. HARRY F. BYRD, Jr., Mr. CHILES, Mr. CURTIS, Mr. DANFORTH, Mr. DOLE, Mr. DOMENICI, Mr. EASTLAND, Mr. GARN, Mr. GOLDWATER, Mr. HANSEN, Mr. HATCH, Mr. HAYAKAWA, Mr. HELMS, Mr. HOLLINGS, Mr. LAXALT, Mr. LUGAR, Mr. McCLELLAN, Mr. McCLURE, Mr. MORGAN, Mr. NUNN, Mr. SCHMITT, Mr. SCOTT, Mr. STEVENS, Mr. STONE, Mr. TALMADGE, Mr. TOWER, Mr. WALLOP, Mr. YOUNG, and Mr. ZORINSKY

JANUARY 18, 1977

Read twice and referred to the Committee on Armed Services

INDEX

All-volunteer force (AVF), 1-2, 16-17, 29, 32, 121, 128, 144

Alternatives to military unions, 40-47, 153-56; *see also* Legislation to prohibit military unions
    armed forces association, 27, 43-44
    bargaining units, 43
    company unions, 147, 155-56
    compulsory national service (CNS), 44-47, 153-54
    conscription, 44-45, 153-54
    force reductions, 42-43, 156
    reassurance through leadership, 41-42
    universal military training, 46-47
    voluntary national service, 45

American Federation of Government Employees (AFGE), 2, 12-14, 22-23, 26, 58-60, 64-65, 69, 130, 149

American Federation of State, County and Municipal Employees (AFSCME), 14

American Servicemen's Union (ASU), 2, 11, 121

Association of Civilian Technicians (ACT), 3, 22, 69, 149; *see also* Reserve forces and unionization

Association, right of; *see also* Constitutional issues
    in the military, 97-100
    in the private sector, 91-92
    in the public sector, 92-94
    in public security forces, 94-95

Codetermination, 13-14, 30-31, 117-18, 120-21, 147; *see also* Western European military unions

Collateral military benefits, erosion of effects of unionization on, 23, 35-36, 135, 150
    and pro-union sentiment in armed forces, 17, 29, 144-45, 154

Collective bargaining, 24, 70-72, 131, 133, 136

Constitutional issues, 36-39, 83-87, 154
    Dash v. *Commanding General, Fort Jackson, S.C.,* 38-39
    Middendorf v. *Henry,* 86, 99
    Parker, Warden et al. v. *Levy,* 37, 83, 86, 97-99, 102
    U.S. v. *Robel,* 103
    U.S. v. *Voorhees,* 38, 86

Effects of unionization on U.S. armed forces, 10, 149-53
    advantages of military unionization, 30-32, 62-64
    disadvantages of military unionization, 32-36
    on functional effectiveness of military, 31-33, 62-63, 72-73, 122, 136-39, 152
    on individual rights and benefits of service personnel, 30, 60, 155
    on political responsiveness of military, 33-35, 73-75, 138, 152-53

Enlisted People's Organizing Committee (EPOC), 3, 69, 149

Foreign policy, influence of military unions on, 57-58

Grievance procedures, effects of unionization on, 18, 28, 150

Inevitability of unionization, 40-41, 155

Legislation to prohibit military unions, 19, 21-22, 82-87, 154-55; *see also* Constitutional issues
    U.S. Senate, *S. 274,* 21, 56, 82, 90
    U.S. Senate, *S. 3079,* 7, 21, 90

Manpower costs and military unionization, 35-36, 57, 150-51

National Association of Government Employees (NAGE), 2-3, 149; *see also* Reserve forces and unionization

Opposition to military unions, conventional, 55-57

Postal union, U.S., 25; *see also* Public

sector unions

effects of unionization on, 22

Public sector unions; *see also* Strike, right or power to
  as analogues of U.S. military unions, 69-73, 130, 139, 145, 149, 156
  evolution of in U.S., 2, 12, 14, 130-31
  and police and fire departments, 2, 69, 131, 149

Reserve forces and unionization, 2, 3, 11, 15, 69, 73, 139

Societal trends and military unionization, 13-15, 125-28, 143-44

Strike, right or power to, 14, 24-25, 28-29, 60, 71-72
  and military unions, 32-33, 151-52, 156
  and police and fire department unions, 25, 57, 69, 73, 131, 149

Uniform Code of Military Justice (UCMJ), 37

Views on military unionization
  absence of consensus in, 143
  of AFGE, 22-23, 134-36
  of commander-in-chief, 18-19, 154
  of Congress, 20-22
  of defense management, 19-20, 136-37, 154
  of military personnel, 15-16, 61, 145
  of military professional associations, 20, 60-61
  of the public, 18, 75-82

Western European military unions, 2, 144
  as analogues of U.S. military unions, 8-9, 23-25, 109-110, 121, 130, 139, 145-48
  in the Federal Republic of Germany, 114, 116, 118, 147-48
  in France, 110-11
  in the Netherlands, 113-115, 147-48
  in Norway, 112-13
  in Sweden, 24-26, 118-21

CONTRIBUTORS

JUDITH A. CROSBY (Ph.D., University of Texas at Austin) is Assistant Professor of Government at Gallaudet College. A specialist in political theory and constitutional law, Dr. Crosby's work has appeared in the *American Jurisprudence Review* and elsewhere.

DAVID Y. DENHOLM (B.A., University of California at Santa Clara) is Executive Vice President of the Public Service Research Council. A career naval reservist, he has written and lectured extensively on public sector unionism.

THEODORE C. HUMES (J.D., George Washington University Law School) is a Staff Counsel to the U.S. Senate Judiciary Committee. He has been an attorney with the Securities and Exchange Commission and a candidate for Congress.

EZRA S. KRENDEL (Sc. M., Massachusetts Institute of Technology; M.A. Harvard University) is Professor of Operations Research at the Wharton School of the University of Pennsylvania. An acknowledged expert on the subject of military unionism, he is co-editor of *Unionizing the Armed Forces.*

CHARLES D. PHILLIPS (Ph.D. candidate, University of Texas at Austin) has been a Policy Analyst at the Federal Judicial Center in Washington, D.C. His work has appeared in a number of professional journals, including the *American Political Science Review*.

COLONEL W. GENE PHILLIPS, USA Ret. (M.S., Southern Illinois University has had extensive experience in labor-management relations in the armed forces. Colonel Phillips has been an influential participant in the discussions on military unionism held by the American Federation of Government Employees.

ALAN NED SABROSKY (Ph.D., University of Michigan) is Assistant Professor of Politics at the Catholic University of America and a Research Associate of the Foreign Policy Research Institute. Dr. Sabrosky's published works include *Defense Manpower Policy: A Critical Reappraisal* and numerous articles in anthologies and professional journals.

COLONEL WILLIAM J. TAYLOR, JR., USA (Ph.D., American University) is Permanent Associate Professor for National Security Studies at the United States Military Academy. Colonel Taylor's work has appeared in numerous books and professional journals, including *Public Administration Review* and the fourth edition of *American Defense Policy*. He is co-authoring a text entitled *The Elements of National Security*.

THOMAS C. WYATT (Ph.D., New York University) is Assistant Professor of Sociology at the George Mason University of Virginia. Dr. Wyatt has taught at the United States Military Academy as well as the U.S. Navy Postgraduate School, and he has written extensively on the subject of military unions over the past five years.